JOMO KENYATTA

JOMO KENYATTA

Dennis Wepman

Library

CHELSEA HOUSE PUBLISHERS
NEW YORK

SENIOR EDITOR: William P. Hansen
ASSOCIATE EDITORS: John Haney
                   Richard Mandell
                   Marian W. Taylor
EDITORIAL COORDINATOR: Karyn Gullen Browne
EDITORIAL STAFF: Jennifer Caldwell
                 Susan Quist
ART DIRECTOR: Susan Lusk
ART ASSISTANTS: Teresa Clark
                Carol McDougall
LAYOUT: Irene Friedman
COVER DESIGN: Beth Russo
PICTURE RESEARCH: Ellen Cibula
                  Leah Malamed
                  Susan Quist

3 5 7 9 8 6 4 2

Library of Congress Cataloging in Publication Data

Wepman, Dennis.
    Jomo Kenyatta.

    (World leaders past & present)
    Bibliography: p.
    Includes index.
    1. Kenyatta, Jomo.   2. Statesmen—Kenya—Biography.
3. Kenya—Presidents—Biography.   I. Title.
II. Series.
DT433.576.K46W46   1985   967.6′204′0924 [B] 84-28506
ISBN 0–87754–575–8
    0-7910-0582-8 (pbk.)

Contents

John Adams
John Quincy Adams
Konrad Adenauer
Alexander the Great
Salvador Allende
Marc Antony
Corazon Aquino
Yasir Arafat
King Arthur
Hafez al-Assad
Kemal Atatürk
Attila
Clement Attlee
Augustus Caesar
Menachem Begin
David Ben-Gurion
Otto von Bismarck
Léon Blum
Simon Bolívar
Cesare Borgia
Willy Brandt
Leonid Brezhnev
Julius Caesar
John Calvin
Jimmy Carter
Fidel Castro
Catherine the Great
Charlemagne
Chiang Kai-Shek
Winston Churchill
Georges Clemenceau
Cleopatra
Constantine the Great
Hernán Cortés
Oliver Cromwell
Georges-Jacques
  Danton
Jefferson Davis
Moshe Dayan
Charles de Gaulle
Eamon De Valera
Eugene Debs
Deng Xiaoping
Benjamin Disraeli
Alexander Dubček
François & Jean-Claude
  Duvalier
Dwight Eisenhower
Eleanor of Aquitaine
Elizabeth I
Faisal
Ferdinand & Isabella
Francisco Franco
Benjamin Franklin

Frederick the Great
Indira Gandhi
Mohandas Gandhi
Giuseppe Garibaldi
Amin & Bashir Gemayel
Genghis Khan
William Gladstone
Mikhail Gorbachev
Ulysses S. Grant
Ernesto "Che" Guevara
Tenzin Gyatso
Alexander Hamilton
Dag Hammarskjöld
Henry VIII
Henry of Navarre
Paul von Hindenburg
Hirohito
Adolf Hitler
Ho Chi Minh
King Hussein
Ivan the Terrible
Andrew Jackson
James I
Wojciech Jaruzelski
Thomas Jefferson
Joan of Arc
Pope John XXIII
Pope John Paul II
Lyndon Johnson
Benito Juárez
John Kennedy
Robert Kennedy
Jomo Kenyatta
Ayatollah Khomeini
Nikita Khrushchev
Kim Il Sung
Martin Luther King, Jr.
Henry Kissinger
Kublai Khan
Lafayette
Robert E. Lee
Vladimir Lenin
Abraham Lincoln
David Lloyd George
Louis XIV
Martin Luther
Judas Maccabeus
James Madison
Nelson & Winnie
  Mandela
Mao Zedong
Ferdinand Marcos
George Marshall

Mary, Queen of Scots
Tomáš Masaryk
Golda Meir
Klemens von Metternich
James Monroe
Hosni Mubarak
Robert Mugabe
Benito Mussolini
Napoléon Bonaparte
Gamal Abdel Nasser
Jawaharlal Nehru
Nero
Nicholas II
Richard Nixon
Kwame Nkrumah
Daniel Ortega
Mohammed Reza Pahlavi
Thomas Paine
Charles Stewart
  Parnell
Pericles
Juan Perón
Peter the Great
Pol Pot
Muammar el-Qaddafi
Ronald Reagan
Cardinal Richelieu
Maximilien Robespierre
Eleanor Roosevelt
Franklin Roosevelt
Theodore Roosevelt
Anwar Sadat
Haile Selassie
Prince Sihanouk
Jan Smuts
Joseph Stalin
Sukarno
Sun Yat-sen
Tamerlane
Mother Teresa
Margaret Thatcher
Josip Broz Tito
Toussaint L'Ouverture
Leon Trotsky
Pierre Trudeau
Harry Truman
Queen Victoria
Lech Walesa
George Washington
Chaim Weizmann
Woodrow Wilson
Xerxes
Emiliano Zapata
Zhou Enlai

CHELSEA HOUSE PUBLISHERS

ON LEADERSHIP

Arthur M. Schlesinger, jr.

LEADERSHIP, it may be said, is really what makes the world go round. Love no doubt smooths the passage; but love is a private transaction between consenting adults. Leadership is a public transaction with history. The idea of leadership affirms the capacity of individuals to move, inspire and mobilize masses of people so that they act together in pursuit of an end. Sometimes leadership serves good purposes, sometimes bad; but whether the end is benign or evil, great leaders are those men and women who leave their personal stamp on history.

Now, the very concept of leadership implies the proposition that individuals can make a difference. This proposition has never been universally accepted. From classical times to the present day, eminent thinkers have regarded individuals as no more than the agents and pawns of larger forces, whether the gods and goddesses of the ancient world or, in the modern era, race, class, nation, the dialectic, the will of the people, the spirit of the times, history itself. Against such forces, the individual dwindles into insignificance.

So contends the thesis of historical determinism. Tolstoy's great novel *War and Peace* offers a famous statement of the case. Why, Tolstoy asked, did millions of men in the Napoleonic wars, denying their human feelings and their common sense, move back and forth across Europe slaughtering their fellows? "The war," Tolstoy answered, "was bound to happen simply because it was bound to happen." All prior history predetermined it. As for leaders, they, Tolstoy said, "are but the labels that serve to give a name to an end and, like labels, they have the least possible connection with the event." The greater the leader, "the more conspicuous the inevitability and the predestination of every act he commits." The leader, said Tolstoy, is "the slave of history."

Determinism takes many forms. Marxism is the determinism of class, Nazism the determinism of race. But the idea of men and women as the slaves of history runs athwart the deepest human instincts. Rigid determinism abolishes the idea of human freedom—the assumption of free choice that underlies every move we make, every word we speak, every thought we think. It abolishes the idea of human responsibility, since it is manifestly unfair to reward or punish people for actions that are by definition beyond their control. No one can live consistently by any deterministic creed. The Marxist states prove this themselves by their extreme susceptibility to the cult of leadership.

More than that, history refutes the idea that individuals make no difference. In December 1931 a British politician crossing Park Avenue in New York City between 76th and 77th Streets around ten-thirty at night looked in the wrong direction and was knocked down by an automobile—a moment, he later recalled, of a man aghast, a world aglare: "I do not understand why I was not broken like an eggshell or squashed like a gooseberry." Fourteen months later an American politician, sitting in an open car in Miami, Florida, was fired on by an assassin; the man beside him was hit. Those who believe that individuals make no difference to history might well ponder whether the next two decades would have been the same had Mario Contasini's car killed Winston Churchill in 1931 and Giuseppe Zangara's bullet killed Franklin Roosevelt in 1933. Suppose, in addition, that Adolf Hitler had been killed in the street fighting during the Munich *Putsch* of 1923 and that Lenin had died of typhus during the First World War. What would the 20th century be like now?

For better or for worse, individuals do make a difference. "The notion that a people can run itself and its affairs anonymously," wrote the philosopher William James, "is now well known to be the silliest of absurdities. Mankind does nothing save through initiatives on the part of inventors, great or small, and imitation by the rest of us—these are the sole factors in human progress. Individuals of genius show the way, and set the patterns, which common people then adopt and follow."

Leadership, James suggests, means leadership in thought as well as in action. In the long run, leaders in thought may well make the greater difference to the world. But, as Woodrow Wilson once said, "Those only are leaders of men, in the general eye, who lead in action. . . . It is at their hands that new thought gets its translation into the crude language of deeds." Leaders in thought often invent in solitude and obscurity, leaving to later generations the tasks of imitation. Leaders in action—the leaders portrayed in this series— have to be effective in their own time.

And they cannot be effective by themselves. They must act in response to the rhythms of their age. Their genius must be adapted, in a phrase of William James's, "to the receptivities of the moment." Leaders are useless without followers. "There goes the mob," said the French politician hearing a clamor in the streets. "I am their leader. I must follow them." Great leaders turn the inchoate emotions of the mob to purposes of their own. They seize on the opportunities of their time, the hopes, fears, frustrations, crises, potentialities.

They succeed when events have prepared the way for them, when the community is waiting to be aroused, when they can provide the clarifying and organizing ideas. Leadership ignites the circuit between the individual and the mass and thereby alters history.

It may alter history for better or for worse. Leaders have been responsible for the most extravagant follies and most monstrous crimes that have beset suffering humanity. They have also been vital in such gains as humanity has made in individual freedom, religious and racial tolerance, social justice and respect for human rights.

There is no sure way to tell in advance who is going to lead for good and who for evil. But a glance at the gallery of men and women in *World Leaders—Past and Present* suggests some useful tests.

One test is this: do leaders lead by force or by persuasion? By command or by consent? Through most of history leadership was exercised by the divine right of authority. The duty of followers was to defer and to obey. "Theirs not to reason why,/ Theirs but to do and die." On occasion, as with the so-called "enlightened despots" of the 18th century in Europe, absolutist leadership was animated by humane purposes. More often, absolutism nourished the passion for domination, land, gold and conquest and resulted in tyranny.

The great revolution of modern times has been the revolution of equality. The idea that all people should be equal in their legal condition has undermined the old structures of authority, hierarchy and deference. The revolution of equality has had two contrary effects on the nature of leadership. For equality, as Alexis de Tocqueville pointed out in his great study *Democracy in America*, might mean equality in servitude as well as equality in freedom.

"I know of only two methods of establishing equality in the political world," Tocqueville wrote. "Rights must be given to every citizen, or none at all to anyone . . . save one, who is the master of all." There was no middle ground "between the sovereignty of all and the absolute power of one man." In his astonishing prediction of 20th-century totalitarian dictatorship, Tocqueville explained how the revolution of equality could lead to the "*Führerprinzip*" and more terrible absolutism than the world had ever known.

But when rights are given to every citizen and the sovereignty of all is established, the problem of leadership takes a new form, becomes more exacting than ever before. It is easy to issue commands and enforce them by the rope and the stake, the concentration camp and the *gulag*. It is much harder to use argument and achievement to overcome opposition and win consent. The Founding Fathers of the United States understood the difficulty. They believed that history had given them the opportunity to decide, as

Alexander Hamilton wrote in the first Federalist Paper, whether men are indeed capable of basing government on "reflection and choice, or whether they are forever destined to depend . . . on accident and force."

Government by reflection and choice called for a new style of leadership and a new quality of followership. It required leaders to be responsive to popular concerns, and it required followers to be active and informed participants in the process. Democracy does not eliminate emotion from politics; sometimes it fosters demagoguery; but it is confident that, as the greatest of democratic leaders put it, you cannot fool all of the people all of the time. It measures leadership by results and retires those who overreach or falter or fail.

It is true that in the long run despots are measured by results too. But they can postpone the day of judgment, sometimes indefinitely, and in the meantime they can do infinite harm. It is also true that democracy is no guarantee of virtue and intelligence in government, for the voice of the people is not necessarily the voice of God. But democracy, by assuring the rights of opposition, offers built-in resistance to the evils inherent in absolutism. As the theologian Reinhold Niebuhr summed it up, "Man's capacity for justice makes democracy possible, but man's inclination to injustice makes democracy necessary."

A second test for leadership is the end for which power is sought. When leaders have as their goal the supremacy of a master race or the promotion of totalitarian revolution or the acquisition and exploitation of colonies or the protection of greed and privilege or the preservation of personal power, it is likely that their leadership will do little to advance the cause of humanity. When their goal is the abolition of slavery, the liberation of women, the enlargement of opportunity for the poor and powerless, the extension of equal rights to racial minorities, the defense of the freedoms of expression and opposition, it is likely that their leadership will increase the sum of human liberty and welfare.

Leaders have done great harm to the world. They have also conferred great benefits. You will find both sorts in this series. Even "good" leaders must be regarded with a certain wariness. Leaders are not demigods; they put on their trousers one leg after another just like ordinary mortals. No leader is infallible, and every leader needs to be reminded of this at regular intervals. Irreverence irritates leaders but is their salvation. Unquestioning submission corrupts leaders and demeans followers. Making a cult of a leader is always a mistake. Fortunately hero worship generates its own antidote. "Every hero," said Emerson, "becomes a bore at last."

The signal benefit the great leaders confer is to embolden the rest of us to live according to our own best selves, to be active, insistent, and resolute in affirming our own sense of things. For great leaders attest to the reality of human freedom against the supposed inevitabilities of history. And they attest to the wisdom and power that may lie within the most unlikely of us, which is why Abraham Lincoln remains the supreme example of great leadership. A great leader, said Emerson, exhibits new possibilities to all humanity. "We feed on genius. . . . Great men exist that there may be greater men."

Great leaders, in short, justify themselves by emancipating and empowering their followers. So humanity struggles to master its destiny, remembering with Alexis de Tocqueville: "It is true that around every man a fatal circle is traced beyond which he cannot pass; but within the wide verge of that circle he is powerful and free; as it is with man, so with communities."

New York

1

Child of the Forest

Kamau wa Ngengi, Kamau son of Ngengi, was about 10 (he never knew his age exactly because the Kikuyu tribe did not record births in those days) when he came down with a serious illness. Living close to the land, always barefoot, he picked up a parasite. Jiggers invaded both feet and spread through one leg. Disease carriers, they gave him a spinal infection that soon threatened his whole body.

His family became frightened. It was about 1905, and the Kikuyu tribe in the village of Ichaweri in East Africa did not have hospitals. Tribal medicine men did what they could—they chanted songs, sacrificed animals, prepared herbal medicines—but nothing helped. Even Kamau's grandfather, Kongo, a seer and magician of the tribe, could not do anything for him. At last the family made a great decision: they would trust their first-born child to the white man's remedies and take him to the Church of Scotland mission at Fort Hall, near Nairobi, 30 miles away.

It was a daring decision for a Kikuyu in those days. The child was terrified. He had never seen a white man, but he had heard horrible stories of the soft, mysterious beings with skin like the bellies of frogs and thundersticks that could shoot fire. He submitted to the treatment with the dumb helplessness of a dog.

No one can doubt that the rich and exceptionally fertile district of Kenya is destined to become one of the chief centers of European cultivation.
—SIR CHARLES ELIOT
leading British administrator in the East African Protectorate

The Masai, nomadic cattle herders, were fierce and highly skilled warriors. They were neighbors of the Kikuyu, who for centuries had been primarily an agricultural people. Although both tribes worshiped the same god, Ngai, and their women frequently traded goods, the Masai and the Kikuyu were for the most part deadly enemies.

German soldiers and settlers establish the West African colony of Cameroon in 1881. There was little European interest in the region until the end of the 19th century, when there began the phenomenon known as the "Scramble for Africa." Initiated by France, the "scramble" soon engaged the governments of Britain, the Netherlands, Belgium, and Germany.

Fortunately, the fearsome whites both cared about their charges and knew their business. Under their treatment Kamau recovered completely. He never forgot their care. Almost 60 years later, when missionaries had few friends in that country, he spoke for them, and his voice saved them from many dangers.

A short time after he was carried into the clinic, the alert child was sitting up watching everything with fascination and asking a thousand questions. He could not learn enough about this strange and powerful new creature, the white man. When he had to return to his village, Kamau already had a sense of a larger world, and perhaps a glimmering of the important role he was to play in it.

The missionary doctors were impressed with the quick mind of the little black boy. They could never have guessed that one day, as Jomo Kenyatta, the "Flaming Spear" of Kenya, he would be called a brutal murderer and a communist, a hero and a savior, and that he would lead his nation to freedom from the white man.

The slopes of these densely forested mountains in Kenya were the home of the Kikuyu tribe, who cleared trees to build villages of round wooden huts with thatched roofs and to cultivate the potatoes, sugar, beans, and bananas which were the staples of their largely vegetarian diet.

Kamau was glad to return to his family and his grass hut in Ichaweri. The Kikuyu are a pastoral tribe, living mainly from their agriculture and cattle, and Kamau went back to herding his father's cows, goats, and sheep and tending the corn and beans in his little patch of garden. He was almost a man now. He had already passed the ritual marking the beginning of a child's economic activities and was expected to take care of his father's herd. He had received his first bow and arrow two years before and could protect the goats from the lions that prowled the area at night. He would soon take his place among the adults of the tribe.

But a glimpse of the world of the whites had planted a seed in the fertile young mind of Kamau, and he could not rest until he knew more. His short stay in the clinic had shown him a thousand mysteries, and he knew even at age 10 that he would be able to command forces greater than those of the most powerful sorcerers and witch doctors if he could acquire the skills he saw as he recuperated.

Other members of his tribe had had contact with whites and had returned gladly to the village. Ichaweri was in a rich area of Kikuyuland southwest of the sacred Mount Kenya. The Europeans held little attraction for the proud, independent Kikuyu, secure on their fertile lands. The Kikuyu were the largest tribe in East Africa, representing more than 20% of the population, and their industry, intelligence, and ambition had made them the richest as well. A gentle, peaceful tribe, they seldom fought except when their land was attacked, but they kept their spears sharp and their leather-covered shields in good repair. There had been wars—with the neighboring Masai, among others—within the memory of some of Kamau's family, and his grandfather Kongo had led troops. The young men of the tribe still danced wild ceremonial dances of blood and death. Kamau had seen them with rattles tied to their legs, leaping high in the air and waving their long spears.

But he had also seen the pale missionaries working their magic with numbers and reading the mysterious printed symbols in books, and heard

Wealthy South African financier Cecil Rhodes (1853-1902) was an energetic colonialist eager to expand the British Empire. Men like Rhodes, whose slogan was "philanthropy plus five percent," had various goals: to win power, make money, and extend "civilization" to Africa, which they often referred to as "the dark continent."

British soldiers disembark at Alexandria, Egypt, in 1915. In 1882 the British had invaded and conquered Egypt, and expansionist South African financier Cecil Rhodes hoped at that time to gain British control of all Africa by building a railway from Egypt to the tip of South Africa.

White settlers watch the construction of a railroad bridge in 1870 in the British colony of Natal, today part of the Republic of South Africa. In the 1890s the British built a railway across Kenya, linking it with the Indian Ocean and thus opening the country for European settlement.

them speak in unknown, unfathomable languages. He had to conquer these secrets. The village and his father's herds could not hold him. He ran away. It was a decision that changed the path of his life—and the history of Africa.

One of the first individualists to break out of his closely knit tribal culture, young Kamau ran back to the mission. He was determined to master the secrets of the white man, to learn to read and write and speak the strange tongue of the missionaries. He convinced the Englishmen to take him in by claiming to be an orphan.

It was an early exercise in politics. The little boy already knew that sometimes you have to bend the truth to get what you want, and he had already begun to develop a gift for convincing people.

The missionaries were happy to find an intelligent native who was interested in learning the ways of the whites. They took him in gladly as a resident student. Their purpose in Africa was to "civilize" the natives by teaching them how to live and think like the English, and young Kamau seemed like promising material. With training, they thought, he could be molded into a useful servant or skilled laborer for the English. They could not have been more wrong.

In 1910, two members of the Kikuyu tribe walk the road to Fort Hall, where the young Kenyatta attended mission school. Until the Europeans appeared, Kikuyu life had remained virtually unchanged for centuries: they were efficient farmers and beekeepers, and lived under an intricate governmental structure based on family units.

2

Mission Boy

The move from Ichaweri to Fort Hall was a change from one world to another and from one age to another. In the 30 miles of tall grass from his village to the mission, Kamau walked from the Stone Age to the dawn of the 20th century. At Fort Hall he learned to wear shoes, to button a shirt, and to use a knife and fork like a European gentleman. By the time he was 13, he could speak English fluently and read and write as well as the average British schoolboy of the same age.

More than that, he had learned to quote the Bible—the main reason the missionaries considered it worth learning to read—and had gained several other equally useful accomplishments. He could play the bugle. He had the rudiments of carpentry. And he could work in a kitchen. He was being equipped to be a good, useful native, one who could repay the devotion of the mission by providing service to the white settlers.

He took it all in for about three years, working at his carpentry and washing dishes and scrubbing floors to pay his way. He read his Bible as regularly as his teachers demanded, but he read everything else he could lay his hands on, too. And he practiced his English at every opportunity, talking to anyone who would listen and spinning long yarns just for the chance to perfect his speech. In fact, one Englishman for whom he worked as a kitchen

The young Kenyatta holds a carpenter's plane, a tool he learned to use at the mission school at Fort Hall. "Mission boys" also learned reading, writing, and arithmetic, despite the misgivings of some families, who feared that such skills were forms of evil magic.

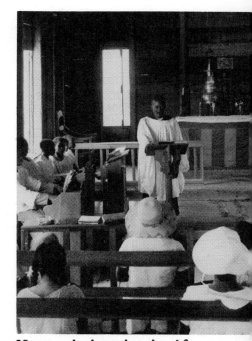

Many missionaries in Africa found making converts to Christianity extremely difficult. The Kikuyu children were often receptive, but older tribe members were reluctant to forsake such traditions as polygamy, ceremonial drinking, and other rituals which were forbidden by most Christian denominations.

hand, hearing him rattle on "like a Chinaman," gave him the nickname John Chinaman at this time.

But his talkative manner was not a true reflection of the intense young Kamau. He was there for a purpose, and he never let himself forget it. He was dedicated to understanding the mind and acquiring the skills of the European. If he had doubts about the mission and the ideas of the whites who ran it, he kept them to himself.

At about age 14, in 1908, he went back home to Ichaweri—not because he was done with the white man's world but because he had not finished with that of the Kikuyu.

His tribe considered the "age-set" a social grouping just as important as the family. An age-set was all those born around the same year—like a graduating class in an American high school. Members of the same age-set were like a club. They were expected to stay together and had certain responsibilities to each other.

It was time for Kamau to return for the initiation ceremonies of his age-set. With those of his age, he was to be formally admitted to his tribe as an adult. This was a solemn event for child and adult alike, and Kamau must have felt some nostalgia for

Lions, rhinoceroses, and leopards roamed the dense forest surrounding the mission school that the young Kenyatta attended. While native students were accustomed to wild animals, newly-arrived missionaries were sometimes startled by the sight of baboons dashing from the woods to raid the Europeans' well tended vegetable gardens.

This Certifies that Mr. Philip A. Casper having paid

to the **MISSIONARY SOCIETY** of the

Methodist Episcopal Church

the sum of **TWENTY DOLLARS**, is hereby constituted A Member **DURING LIFE** conformally

to the SEVENTH ARTICLE of the CONSTITUTION.

New York. May 10th 1848.

Edmund S. Janes Chairman

Benjamin Edwards Clerk.

Christian missionaries, both European and American, flocked to Africa in the 19th century, bringing "the message of salvation to those who bowed down to wood and stone." Besides providing religious instruction, the missionaries established hospitals, taught modern farming methods, and helped end such backward practices as the ritual killing of twin babies.

the old ways. Like a Jewish boy's bar mitzvah or a Catholic's confirmation, the coming-of-age ritual was a turning point in the life of a Kikuyu. Three years in the mission had not so Europeanized Kamau that he had lost his Kikuyu identity.

Along with his contemporaries, both boys and girls, he went through all the steps. His ears were pierced, his head shaved, and his face marked with white earth. He took part in the Great Dance, raced the other boys to the sacred fig tree, and took the tribal oath. Then, with the others, he was sprayed with honey, milk, and medicines. At last, cleansed and anointed, he underwent the sacred ritual that made him an adult member of the tribe. Dressed in the traditional goatskin, he received the iron spear, the bush knife, and the buffalo-hide shield of a warrior and took his place facing Mount Kenya, the sacred mountain, home of the tribal deity Ngai. Here he made the final vow and became a man among the Kikuyu.

Back among his own people, Kamau returned to the life of the tribe. His father gave him some sheep and a plot of land to work, and he cultivated

The young Kenyatta's mission school was one of many such outposts established by Catholic and Protestant missionaries in Africa. By 1900 more than 4 million Africans had been converted to Christianity; many of them had also been educated in reading, writing, and arithmetic and also in the most modern sanitation and agricultural techniques.

corn and beans and millet like everyone else. And soon he met a girl from his own age-set. His father paid 34 sheep to her family for her, and she became Kamau's wife. He was now the head of a household.

He must have had some doubts about his real place, though. He worked his plot in the rich highlands of Kikuyuland, but part of his spirit must have remained with the white missionaries who had exposed him to the great world outside. Evidently Kamau, like many Africans exposed to European culture and Christianity, felt somewhat unsure of where he belonged and what he believed. Part of him was still faithful to Ngai, but the god of the missionaries claimed a part too, and soon after his tribal wedding he took his bewildered bride into Nyeri for a second ceremony at the Presbyterian church there.

Standing with a foot in each of two worlds can be an uncomfortable position. Increasingly Kamau found himself restless on his little plot of land, and gradually he began drifting back to Fort Hall to continue his studies. Working as a houseboy for

This very night you are to go and strike the blow and then die.... This is the only way to show the white man that the treatment they are treating our men and women was most bad and we have decided to strike a first and a last blow, and then all die by the heavy storm of the white man's army. The white men will then think, after we are dead, that the treatment they are treating our people is almost bad, and they might change.
—JOHN CHILEMBWE
early 20th-century rebel against white rule in Africa

"White hunters," like this European marksman costumed in solar topee, breeches, and boots, became a symbol of the often arrogant and sometimes cruel settlers who ruled Africa for almost a century.

Had he not chosen to receive a European-style education and, later, to travel abroad, the future Jomo Kenyatta would have taken his place in the ranks of Kikuyu warriors like these. Basically a peaceful agrarian people, the Kikuyu were also brave fighters when provoked.

an English settler, he studied mathematics and English and continued to work at carpentry. A girl who was studying there at the same time remembered him later as unlike the others—a serious boy with no time for joking or girls.

The skills which his years in Ichaweri had sharpened—keen observation and verbal memory, so necessary to a life close to nature in a tribe with no writing system—were valuable to him now. He mastered not only English but Swahili, the principal

General Paul von Lettow-Vorbeck (1870-1964), commander of Germany's forces in East Africa during World War I. This brilliant and resourceful soldier held out against Allied forces until the war's end with an efficient, integrated army of 11,000 African and 2,200 German servicemen, thus exploding élitist myths of the natives' lesser intelligence.

trade language in East Africa and the one most widely used between tribes. His gift for languages was to enable him to acquire several others.

He was a star pupil, and the missionary teachers, misreading his real character completely, considered him one of their great successes. In 1914, when he was about 20, they made his acceptance into their world official by baptizing him, giving him a good, solid English name. From that day, in the eyes of the English his "real" name was Johnstone Kamau. It was almost like being an Englishman.

But his natural intelligence and the powers of observation cultivated on the land were not dulled by his life at the mission. He thanked his teachers and he paid his way with his work, but he was not deceived by their benevolence. He learned to read and write from them, and he also learned to see the two cultures in perspective. He gave them what they wanted, but he saw through them and realized that they were in Africa not to elevate its culture but to destroy it and substitute their own. At 20 he decided it was time to push on. He had gotten all that the Church of Scotland mission had to give him.

Short of native bearers, the German army in Africa forced many Africans— men and women—to work as porters in World War I. The casualties, due to overwork and disease, were enormous. One witness reported that the carriers were often roped together and "shot indiscriminately if they tried to escape."

3

Kikuyu Shepherd

Life in the village was limited, but Kamau felt bound to it. He cultivated the lands provided by his father, and now he had his own family to support.

The family of Ngengi, Kamau's father, was not one of the great, powerful ones, but they were reasonably well-off. There was enough land to provide food, and sheep, goats, and cows for meat and milk. If the English government had left the native population alone and left the laws as they were then, East Africa might still be a protectorate of England and the descendants of Kamau might still be peacefully tilling its soil.

But in 1915 a new law made a peaceful life for the Kikuyu impossible. It so shattered the security of these pastoral natives that trouble was inevitable. Relations between the English and the Africans, never exactly warm and cordial, were fatally affected by it. More than any single decision, it probably brought about the end of English rule in Africa.

The law, called the Crown Lands Ordinance, declared that Africans had no legal right to own land. Basically, it limited the possession of land to English whites, and its effect on the social and economic lives of the native populace of East Africa was devastating.

The Crown Lands Ordinance of 1915 was a particular blow to the Kikuyu because of the particular importance land had for them. When the Kikuyu

British architect Sir Herbert Baker (1862-1946). Once called "the most thoroughly imperial of all the imperial architects," Baker designed many official buildings in Africa and India, including Government House in Nairobi. His majestic formal buildings, constructed in classic European style, reflected little of the culture of the colonial territories in which they were built.

Kikuyu girls display the intricate costume worn for the ceremony initiating them as adults. Kikuyu women were traditionally made responsible not only for planting the less important crops but also for all cultivation, weeding, and harvesting.

King of Great Britain from 1910 to 1936, George V (1865-1936) was a thoroughgoing imperialist who regarded the British Empire as permanent. Shown here with his wife, Queen Mary, George V thought that independence for most colonies would be difficult because of "the utter lack of courage, moral or political, among the natives."

first arrived in this area some centuries before, there were no other tribes there. They peacefully occupied the north and central parts of their present districts and bought adjacent land to the south from the Dorodo tribe. These parcels of land were measured and recorded as clearly as the real estate of any city in England or the United States. The nine major clans of the Kikuyu were divided into sub-clans or extended families, and each of them was formally assigned rights over particular pieces of property.

Definite tribal laws governed this ownership. The plots could be sold or rented or inherited only according to rules clearly defined in tribal law. These laws were centuries old, and had been recognized and respected by the Kikuyu and their neighbors since long before the first white men had come.

When the English first arrived in the 1890s, they passed their own laws. Like the Kikuyu centuries before, they simply occupied and claimed empty land, or land they thought to be empty. In order to maintain a European sense of order and control, they assumed legal control over the whole area, and in 1895 proclaimed it the East African Protectorate.

In an effort at assuring a just treatment of the natives, the English established a rule against the claim of any land "regularly utilized by Africans." But the law was not very clearly defined, and as the English people learned what rich, fertile farming land there was in East Africa, they flocked over. It became harder and harder to protect native landowners, and the English government did little to keep to the spirit of its earlier promise to do so.

The Kikuyu, as pastoral and agricultural people, were the greatest sufferers. One by one they were pushed out of their ancestral homes with the excuse that they weren't farming correctly or utilizing the land efficiently. Always under the protection of their own laws, the English claimed more and more of the best lands, rejecting Kikuyu protest in their courts. The official explanation for this rejection was stated very clearly in a court case upholding a settler's claim in 1919: "The theory of individual ownership of land as understood in English is absolutely foreign to the mind of any African."

With such an understanding of the African mind, it was easy for the English to justify the Crown Lands Ordinance of 1915. The English never doubted from the beginning of their settlement in the area that it would eventually all become theirs.

Much of the best farmland had already been acquired, by 1915, through tricky "purchases" much like the purchase of American Indian lands in North America. The choice Chura and Limuru areas, for example, were owned by 11,000 Kikuyu, but the British government took it for settlers, compensating 8,000 of them with a total of 8,000 shillings, then worth about $1,920. This came to less than 25¢ each for those who were paid; the remaining

Bonar Law (1858-1923) was Britain's colonial secretary from 1915 to 1916. Never deeply concerned about the empire's native populations, Law presided over the passage of the notorious Crown Lands Ordinance of 1915, which deprived many thousands of Kenyans (including the Kikuyu) of their traditional, and often sacred, holdings.

British colonial administrator Francis Hall (at far right) once called the Kikuyu "very treacherous." His attitude was typical of that held by many white men about Africans at the time. One historian noted that, to such men, "the idea that the interests of barbaric tribesmen should be exalted above those of the educated European would [seem] fantastic."

3,000 natives received nothing at all.

When natives protested, the English sent out military expeditions to "pacify" them—that is, to hunt the troublemakers down like game. An account of such an expedition in a letter by Francis Hall, the Crown administrator for whom Fort Hall was named, gives an idea of the spirit in which such expeditions were carried out:

"We scoured the forest . . . sending columns out to burn the villages and collect goats, etc. We rarely saw any of the people; when we did, they were at long range, so we did not have much fun, but we destroyed a tremendous number of villages."

The English upper classes have always had a taste for hunting, and an army takes its fun where it finds it. Unfortunately, the Kikuyu did not often enter into the spirit of the game.

When the Crown Lands Ordinance was passed in 1915, it left the tribes with no property of their own. They were permitted to stay on their farms only at the will of the English, who could resettle them on reservations like the Indian reservations in the United States. These institutions, which have been compared to concentration camps, soon became impossibly overcrowded and unable to support their growing populations. Many cases of starvation were reported.

The Africans had no choice but to move to the slums of the city or to work for starvation wages on settlers' farms. Once-proud landowners became field hands for settlers who had merely taken over their farms. Norman Leys, in his 1924 book *Kenya*, estimated that in 1920 more than 50% of the able-bodied men in the country from agricultural tribes worked as field hands for Europeans. In a quarter of a century, the English had created a feudal system and a landed aristocracy which dominated millions of serfs.

Kamau's family was not affected by these government appropriations, but everywhere around him he saw what was happening, and he could not have been unaware of the inevitable breakdown of

Students at Eton, an exclusive English prep school, drill with wooden rifles during World War I. In their imperial heyday the British were quick to meet every instance of trouble with guns, as voiced in a once-popular slogan—"Put your trust in God and keep your powder dry."

In the late 19th and early 20th centuries big-game hunting in Africa was a fashionable pastime. This U.S. politician and hunter, George Tinkham, boasted in 1923 that he had killed an elephant, a rhinoceros, a buffalo, a lion, six leopards, a cheetah and "several varieties of deer and antelope" in the course of a single expedition.

the Kikuyu way of life. Protests came from all sides, usually cautiously presented, and there was even some support for the Kikuyu position in England.

Because land was more important to the herding and farming Kikuyu than to other tribes, and because theirs were the greatest and best land holdings in East Africa, they were more affected by the Ordinance than any others. It is not surprising that the proud and enterprising Kikuyu were responsible for most of the lawsuits protesting appropriations.

In 1920, Chief Kioi started a big land case against the settlers. Kamau was the son of a landowner, and, more important, as the first-born son he was a *moramati*, a trustee of the family lands. This meant that he had been brought up with a full knowledge of tribal law regarding land tenure, the rights to land. Perhaps most important of all, he was one of the few Kikuyu who were really fluent in both Swahili and English. Chief Kioi asked the young man to serve as his interpreter in the case.

There is no reason to think that Kamau had given any serious thought to the injustices done to his people before this, or that he had felt any ambitions as a leader. But this case, hopeless as he soon saw it to be, engaged his mind and his feelings, and he argued as passionately as if he had been pleading his own case. The English heard the case in the *Kiama*, the local court, and in 1921 the supreme court in Nairobi listened politely before throwing it out of court, along with all the others. It was not a remarkable case—just one of many in which the supreme court in Nairobi upheld the Crown Lands Ordinance. But it was the beginning of the future Jomo Kenyatta's public career, and perhaps it directed his mind for the first time toward the main social and economic problem of his people.

Whether or not it directed his thoughts anywhere, it directed his feet. His experience in the capital, unsuccessful though it was, opened his eyes to the possibilities that a big city held for him. Once more it was time to move on—this time to a place where his skills and talents might have an outlet. At about 26, he was ready for the larger world he had heard about at the mission school.

British soldier and leading imperialist Horatio Kitchener (1850-1916). In 1911 Kitchener requested free Crown lands in Kenya from his old friend Sir Percy Girouard, the governor of the colony. Girouard promptly gave General Kitchener and two partners 9,000 acres of prime land that had previously been a favorite tribal grazing area.

In the early 1900s, Nairobi, Kenya's capital and political and business center, was not unlike an American frontier town. Most of the rickety houses were made of wood or corrugated tin, open sewers ran down the sides of the streets, and music halls and casinos provided entertainment.

4

Man about Town

Nairobi, the capital of the newly declared Kenya colony, was a young city. It had been a camp for East Indians building the British railroad a few years before and now was a busy, growing shantytown sprawling among swamps between the Masai grazing land to the east and the Kikuyu country to the north and west. In 1907 it had replaced Mombasa as the capital of the East African Protectorate, and if it was not much of a town by modern standards, it was already the city of opportunity for ambitious East Africans.

Mr. Johnstone Kamau, mission-educated and highly cultured compared to the people he had left behind in Ichaweri, arrived in this bustling frontier town with all his possessions in a bag. His ambitions were modest enough—he was under no illusions about what was available to him as a native African, and he just wanted to make some money and enjoy the life of the city.

His talents and skills were sufficient to guarantee that much, and he had no trouble picking up odd jobs. With an ability at mathematics and his command of English and Swahili, along with several tribal dialects of the region, he was a highly qualified worker. He got a job for the city reading water meters, and soon attained the exalted post of water supply inspector—about as high as a black man could hope to go in Nairobi, where all important government jobs were held by English whites

Great and wise and wonderful is the European/He came into our land with his wisdom and might/He made wars to cease/He causes our fields to bring forth plenty/And our flocks to increase/He gives us great riches, and then—/He takes them all away again in taxes/Great and wise and wonderful is the European
—song popular with poor black Nairobi workers during the 1920s

British statesman Winston Churchill (1874-1965) was undersecretary for colonial affairs when he visited Kenya in 1907. Profoundly distressed by the excessively harsh attitude of the white settlers toward the colony's native population, Churchill consistently opposed the settlers' demands for self-rule.

Nairobi water-meter reader Jomo Kenyatta poses with his bicycle and friends in 1921. He later acquired a motorcycle, still considered "new-fangled" in Nairobi, where electricity had only recently been installed. A rhinoceros once caused a serious citywide blackout when it rambled through a power plant.

"What strange-looking people!" It is difficult to tell which group—the Kikuyu or the Europeans—is more puzzled by the other. Frederick Lugard, a British adventurer and colonial agent who encountered the Kikuyu in 1890, observed that they were "extremely intelligent, good mannered, and *most* friendly."

I sympathize profoundly with the native races whose land it was long before we came here, but I don't believe in politics for them .... When I consider their political future I must say that I look into shadows and darkness.

—GENERAL JAN SMUTS
South African soldier and statesman

and all business and skilled labor was in the hands of Asians.

As an employee in the public works department, he had both a good salary and a high status, and the evidence suggests that he enjoyed it all thoroughly. To be sure, he still had to live in an African reserve, a black ghetto for natives, outside the town, but he did not seem to mind; in fact, he apparently raised as much hell as the law allowed. A big man with a commanding presence, he was a well-known figure in the Nairobi African reserve in those days. His old friend and fellow activist, Mbui Koinange, remembered him as quite a dandy:

"He used to wear a large cowboy felt hat with its band decorated by beads. . . a half-sleeve khaki jacket with four pockets all with flaps. Around the waist was a huge beaded belt fastened with a large copper buckle to match, a pair of riding breeches and a pair of light brown boots."

In this outfit, he roared out to his ghetto home after work every night on his powerful motorcycle. He lived lustily, drinking with his friends and chasing women. The indignity of his situation—the fact that he could not enter a "white" hotel or restaurant, that he was a second-class citizen of his own country—made little impression on him in his first year in Nairobi. If he felt any indignation about his social position or that of his fellow Kikuyu, he did not advertise the fact.

In a short time, feeling the need for a home and a woman on a regular basis, he took a second wife. This was not unusual among Kikuyu who could afford it; his father, Ngengi, had several, and it is said that his first wife in Ichaweri even suggested the move.

He was now a complete city man, and along with his new life he took a new name. He had outgrown Kamau, his village name, but he had not left his Kikuyu identity behind. The white, red, green, and black beaded belt he habitually wore was a Kikuyu item of apparel, and he took the name Kenyatta, the Kikuyu word for it, as his own. It was now as Johnstone Kenyatta that he lived and worked, drank and played, in Nairobi.

Life was good for him. He had money, a wife, a good job, and no problems. The problems of his country and his people were not his problems. He was, according to his younger brother, Moigai, simply "not interested in politics."

Other people in Nairobi were, however. In 1920, the year that saw the change of status from a protectorate to a colony for Kenya, other changes affected the lives of the people, all of them for the worse. As colonials, natives were charged both a poll tax and a hut tax. During 1920 both of these taxes were doubled, and a fingerprinted I.D. card was issued to all African males over 15, which they were required to carry at all times on penalty of imprisonment. In 1921 farm wages were cut by

Blank, brutal, uninteresting, amorphous barbarism.
—description of native culture made by an early 20th-century British administrator in the East African Protectorate

British dignitaries prepare to meet tribal chieftains at Freetown, Sierra Leone, in 1925. Standing at left (reading a pamphlet) is the Prince of Wales, the future King Edward VIII. Edward greatly dismayed Britain's ruling classes in 1936 when he abdicated in order to marry American socialite Mrs. Wallis Simpson.

Three young British subjects chat on a hillside overlooking the British naval base at Simonstown, South Africa, in 1915. It was largely through its enormous navy that Britain acquired what poet Rudyard Kipling (1865-1936) called "dominion over palm and pine"—the far-flung British Empire.

one-third to keep native laborers from accumulating enough money to escape. Worst of all, the uncompensated appropriations of farmland for European settlers increased.

The "theft of the land" was what hurt most, of course. As Kenyatta was to write many years later, "The question of land tenure . . . is the key to the people's life." Murmurings of complaint began to be heard everywhere, at all levels of society. The loss was not only economic, although poverty was the most obvious result. The damage was spiritual and psychological as well. Kenyatta wrote in 1938:

"Land is the most important factor in the social, political, and religious life of the tribe. . . . Communion with the ancestral spirits is perpetuated through contact with the soil in which the ancestors of the tribe lie buried."

In 1920 Kenyatta had not yet begun to concern himself with these problems, at least not in an active way. But the yeast of rebellion was beginning to bubble around him, and, even in his fun-filled first year in Nairobi, he must have heard something of it.

Near the capital, mass meetings were being held in Kikuyu territory by Harry Thuku, a man historians have called "the first undisputed hero of the politically conscious Kikuyu." Thuku, a member of one of the richest and most influential Kikuyu families, had been born around the same year as Kamau, and like him had spent some time at a mission school. At 20, he had gotten a job as a typesetter on an English-language newspaper because he was one of the few people of his tribe who could read and write the language. In 1918 he moved still further up in the world. He got a job as a telephone operator in the treasury department.

Government jobs were very rare for black Africans, and it is probable that he and the flamboyant Kenyatta met in those days. But while the water inspector was racing around on his motorcycle, the telephone operator was using his position on the telephone exchange to uncover the secrets of the colonial government, and with this information was trying to arouse native feeling to protest.

Thuku was not completely alone in his work. The East Indian community of Kenya also had grievances, and was engaged in its own struggle with England for racial equality. Though some of them were wealthy, the Indians, like the blacks, were forced to live in ghettos, and they too were denied the rights of land ownership or a chance at the best jobs. At the same time as Gandhi was openly fighting for self-determination for India, the Indians in Africa were asking only for equal rights. An Indian newspaper, *The East African Chronicle,* supported Thuku's efforts and gave him the use of an office and a car. They felt that whatever he accomplished for justice among the blacks would work for them, too.

Organizations began springing up everywhere. In 1920 the Kikuyu Association, made up mostly of chiefs worried about the loss of their lands and the compulsory labor policies, was formed in Nairobi. The next year Thuku set up the much broader-based Young Kikuyu Association, composed mainly of city people—government clerks, office boys, and servants.

The YKA had a five-point program. With mass meetings and petitions, they protested against the Crown Lands Ordinance, the appropriations of

The nomadic and warlike Masai inspired both fear and contempt among the European settlers. Leading British colonialist Charles Eliot perhaps spoke for many of his countrymen when in 1910 he said, "Masaidom is a beastly, bloody system.... The sooner it disappears, the better."

Kikuyu lands, the increase in taxes, the reduction of wages, and the humiliating I.D. cards which blacks were forced to wear around their necks in plain view.

In the following months, Thuku organized the first multi-tribal group, the East African Association, aimed at uniting all Kenya tribes and protesting all the grievances of black Africa. Composed mostly of Kikuyu, the EAA complained most loudly about the government's theft of Kikuyu land. Thuku urged the people to refuse to work for Europeans, and, like the American draft-card burnings of the 1960s, to throw their I.D. cards on the lawns of Government House in Nairobi.

Of course, Thuku could not be allowed to stir up the natives. The government, with its usual insensitivity to public feeling, arrested him in March, 1922, on charges of being "dangerous to peace and good order." It was a fair charge—Thuku was certainly dangerous to *their* peace and good order—but it was the worst mistake they could have made. This arrogant arrest of a popular hero triggered a reaction whose reverberations did not die away till the English had been driven out of Kenya.

At once the first general strike in Kenya's history took place. Thousands of Africans, mostly Kikuyu, gathered spontaneously at the jail where Thuku was being held and demanded that he be set free.

The women were especially excited. Kikuyu women are famous for their independent minds, and those in the crowd began taunting the men. A witness, Job Muchuchu, reported:

"Mary Nyanjiru leapt to her feet, pulled her dress right up over her shoulders and shouted to the men: 'You take my dress and give me your trousers.

The British settlers who fell in love with the lush lands of East Africa greatly enjoyed appropriating such territory. A British colonial official called it "a white man's country," explaining that he could "say this with no thought of injustice to any native race, for the country is either utterly uninhabited ... or its inhabitants are wandering hunters."

You men are cowards. What are you waiting for? Our leader is in there. Let's get him.' Mary and the others pushed on until the bayonets . . . were pricking at their throats, and then the firing started. Mary was one of the first to die."

With the settlers on the hotel veranda joining in the shooting, 56 Africans were brought down in a few minutes. The newspapers reported 25 deaths, four of them women and one a boy.

The governor of the colony, Sir Edward Northey, wrote to England, "By next morning everything was normal . . . proof that the majority of the crowd attended out of curiosity." The English still did not see any handwriting on the wall. But feelings were running high, and everyone knew it except the government. They deported Thuku and restricted him to a desert village. They also broke up the meetings of his followers with bullets, but the tide was gradually rising. Some time in 1922, Jomo Kenyatta joined the EAA.

Kikuyu leaders such as these were chosen for various personal attributes: seniority, the respect they earned from their fellows, and the number of wives or lands they possessed. One historian has noted that Kikuyu government was "perhaps the nearest Africa came to democratic rule in precolonial days."

5

Activist

Harry Thuku's arrest took place on March 14, 1922. Just four days earlier the British had arrested Mohandas K. Gandhi in India on similar charges. Clearly something was in the air, and the British government had no way of responding to it except with arrest warrants and guns.

But popular sympathy and support are not usually won by iron-fist tactics, and violent repression of protest usually turns more people against a government than it attracts.

The reaction to the Nairobi massacre was worldwide. Even in England there was more sympathy for the Kikuyu than for the colonial administration. Future prime minister Winston Churchill, then colonial secretary, had been one of the first to sense the danger of the British position, and had tried to introduce more humane laws in Kenya, if only from practical considerations. As early as 1907 he wrote of Kenya, "There are already . . . all the elements of keen racial and political discord." Now, 15 years later, he was being proved right. But no one seemed able to stop the momentum.

Three months after the massacre, in June, Governor Northey was abruptly recalled to England and Sir Roger Coryndon, then governor of Uganda, put in his place. An idea of public sentiment about the colony can be glimpsed from Coryndon's telegram to a friend: "Have accepted governorship of Kenya. No more peace."

David Lloyd George (1863-1945), premier of Great Britain from 1916-1922, headed the British delegation to Versailles, France, where, in 1919, the treaty ending World War I was signed and the League of Nations created. The British prevented the inclusion of a clause in that organization's charter which declared all races equal.

Wearing one of his trademark hats, the future president of Kenya, still known as Johnstone Kenyatta, poses in 1925 with his wife, Grace Wahu, and their small son, Peter Muigai, named for Kenyatta's father. At right is Kenyatta's half-brother, James Muigai.

We can not know for sure what drew the flashy, high-living Kenyatta to the EAA in 1922. He had been acting occasionally as an interpreter for the high court in Nairobi, so he had seen some of the working of the justice system, and he had earlier been involved with Chief Kioi's unsuccessful effort at gaining justice from that system. Maybe it was just that the fundamental insult of his status as a black man in a white-dominated colony finally became intolerable.

The English, of course, acted with what they saw as not only justice but generosity. They saw themselves as the proud guardians of a superior civilization which they were trying to share with the poor black savages of Africa. They had no doubt that their values and customs were the highest yet achieved by man. A government document of 1921 makes this quite clear. It describes colonization as a sacred responsibility for which the British race had prepared itself "by centuries of evolution."

It is difficult to fight against such a position as this. If the argument were simply about ownership of property between equals, a court might judge fairly; but when the two sides represent "civilization" and "savagery," it is hard to get equal consideration—especially in the courts of the country that considers itself civilized.

Kenyatta's knowledge of languages and his experience with the courts and the government made

British settlers inspect the crops on their African plantation in the early 1900s. As increasing numbers of European planters settled in Africa, they appropriated farmlands which Africans had cultivated for generations, forcing them to move to the much less fertile "native reserve" areas.

Kikuyu villages consisted of clusters of huts; in each cluster was one building for the head of the family, another for each of his wives and her children, still another for each of his older sons. Other huts were often used to store crops.

him a valuable member of the EAA. With its main figures gone after the arrest of Harry Thuku and other leaders, the group was floundering and keeping a low profile. In fact, it was almost an underground organization at this time, and membership in it was seen as a dangerous affair. It was especially risky for Kenyatta, because he was a civil servant and thus not permitted to engage in political activities.

The EAA seems to have operated under different names, and various sources give different accounts of its leadership. It issued statements and made demands, but it accomplished little except to get everyone involved into the police files. By 1924 there is a record that Fort Hall notified the Nairobi government police that Kenyatta was a "dangerous agitator" to be watched. It was obviously just a matter of time before such a dramatic personality as Jomo Kenyatta would bring the law down on his head and that of his organization. As its propaganda chief, he called as much attention to it as he could, and in 1925 the government ordered it disbanded. Almost without stopping for breath, the group reorganized as the Kikuyu Central Association.

For 16 years the KCA agitated openly—and for a few more years it worked underground—for the same series of causes. It was never a very large group, but it became a potent voice, and finally was the only voice, of native Kenya. Until its abolition by the government it remained the only effec-

During those early years from 1893 onwards Mr. Hall taught the Kikuyu the lesson of obedience and instilled in them an implicit faith in the promises of Government.
—British political report on Francis Hall, a leading administrator during the early years of white settlement in Kenya who greatly enjoyed enforcing native obedience at gunpoint

British prime minister Ramsay MacDonald (1866-1937) headed the Labor party, which during the 1920s contained many intellectuals sympathetic to the plight of the empire's subject races. Laborite hopes for radical change in British colonial policies were shattered when MacDonald abandoned his party in 1931, thus briefly depriving it of direction.

tive force for the Kikuyu.

Kenyatta's exact position in this somewhat shadowy organization during this period is not completely clear. He was still an employee of the department of public works, he could not speak out or work too openly for the KCA. If he—or, indeed, the KCA—did anything significant in these years, it was not apparent. The colonial office in London and the government in Nairobi never gave an inch; in fact they added new problems to the already burdened life of the natives.

The KCA continued to ask for return of, or reasonable compensation for, their lands. They tried to get permission to grow cash crops, like coffee, which the settlers refused to let them do. They argued for relief of the poll and hut taxes, especially for women, who were driven into prostitution by them. They fought against the hated I.D. cards which all African men had to carry. And they pleaded for representation in the government and public schools for their children.

The government wisely let them blow off steam by talking about these issues, but politely ignored their petitions and rallies. It was not until 1928 that a real confrontation occurred on one issue that gave the KCA a chance to force a change.

The conflict was not with the government but with the missions. The Christian missionaries had steadily opposed polygamy—the custom of taking more than one wife, common among the Kikuyu—but nothing had been done about it. Now they began to take a strong stand against polygamy, as well as against other native customs, and the conflict came into the open.

The missionaries considered their first duty to be to spread Christianity. Around 1928 they began to speak very strongly against anything that did not conform to Christian tradition. This included all "pagan" songs and dances, the coming-of-age ceremony, indeed everything that defined Kikuyu culture. Those whose families persisted in these pagan practices were barred from the mission schools, the only schools there were for Africans.

Thus the price for education, or any other benefit of the church, was total rejection of the tribal culture.

Here was an issue the KCA could get its teeth into. The new missionary administration was so inflexible that they could not make any concessions: once they declared a thing "pagan" or "savage" they could not relent and work out a compromise between native tradition and Christian dogma. It was all or nothing.

But the missionaries did not have guns or prisons, so the natives could speak out clearly and strongly without fear that a Francis Hall could get them within the range of his rifle. It was a chance to drive a wedge between African and Englishman without starting a politically dangerous rebellion. The KCA did not pass it up.

At once people began to organize a new school movement—one free of any contact with missionaries or any other Europeans. And as education was mixed in the people's minds with religion, a new church began to emerge with it.

The Kikuyu Independent Schools Association (KISA), and the African Independent Pentecostal Church, which fused orthodox Christianity with

The first rails of the Imperial British East Africa Company's railroad, which opened eastern Africa to British settlement, were laid at the Indian Ocean port city of Mombasa in 1895. Beset by hostile tribes, disease, and predators, the building of this remarkable, 700-mile line took more than five years.

Kikuyu tribal traditions, became the focal points for the growing anti-European feeling of young Africans. It was the chance the KCA had waited for, and they made the most of it. Legal means of getting their rights—the endless unsuccessful lawsuits and the pointless petitions the government ignored—had been fruitless and frustrating. The law was a dead end: the settlers and the colonial administration were too strong and were set against them. Now they had a platform based on culture and religion, and the public was ready to move.

The new schools and the new church bred others; another school movement and another church group, even more militant and aggressive, formed in competition. But if they couldn't agree with each other, they all agreed in opposing the missions. In the next couple of years the effects were spectacular. The KCA's inflammatory speeches drew natives away from the mission schools and congregations in droves. The Church of Scotland mission in Kikuyu province lost 90% of its members, and the Africa Inland Mission even more.

By 1931 the European churches had backed down—a face-saving compromise they could live with—and regained a large part of their congregation. But European authority, religious or political, would never be quite the same.

Kenyatta's theatrical personality was made to order for this sort of confrontation. His public appearances drew huge crowds, and his speeches in Kikuyu and Swahili held them spellbound. He was a product of the missions himself, so he knew what he was talking about. All the hypocrisy he had quietly observed at Fort Hall he now emphasized.

He had not forgotten what the missionaries had done for him—without them he would be dead or still hoeing beans and herding goats at Ichaweri—nor had he missed the real purpose underlying their kindness and helpfulness to him. It all came back to the land—the eternal, central, burning issue. It was only this that really mattered to anyone—the beautiful, rich, fertile land of Kenya. The administrators had taken it with their guns and their law books, and the missionaries had backed the administrators up with their schools and their Bibles. Now was his chance to speak out for his people, his continent. Johnstone Kenyatta, half of his name still a survival of his mission days but the other half pure Kikuyu, had found a voice.

Kenyatta and the KCA were not, as the missions charged, rejecting Christianity. They were only calling for the preservation of Kikuyu culture. They did it by every means they had: they organized public rallies, they sponsored and supported schools, and in 1928 they started the first Kikuyu-language newspaper and the first periodical published by Africans for Africans in that area.

Muigwithania ("the Unifier" or "the Reconciler") came out monthly. Edited and largely written by Kenyatta, it was eagerly awaited by every literate Kikuyu. On the surface, it was strictly practical—it had advice on planting fruit trees and bringing up children; it urged people to go to school and to keep their homes clean. It reported KCA meetings and government announcements. It was full of riddles and proverbs, stories and songs, from Kikuyu tradition.

It was all very mild and gentle and carefully writ-

A European official inspects an integrated mission school in Africa during the early 1900s. Because European colonial governments had no budgets or personnel with which to operate schools, missionaries, assisted by their more literate converts, were the earliest purveyors of basic education to the continent's children.

ten to avoid offending the government and giving them the chance to move against the KCA. But if the government did not get the idea, the readers did. The name *Muigwithania* itself was the tip-off—its real objective was to unify its readers. Its riddles and proverbs brought its readers together in the shared experience of their tribe. Every folktale reminded the Kikuyu who read it that he *was* a Kikuyu and gave him pride in it. It did not have to cry out "Get rid of the European!" Every recipe and folk song and proverb hinted it.

Kenyatta ran *Muigwithania* for most of its first year. The proof that he established a style the KCA could get away with was that it lasted, with occasional lapses, until the beginning of World War II. The government did not like it—they did not like the idea of the Kikuyu having their own forum—but they never found an excuse for closing it down. So it continued quietly doing its work for over a decade.

Its importance for Kenyatta was that it gave him a platform from which to address the nation. He quickly emerged like a butterfly from its cocoon into the bright, clear sunlight of Nairobi. He had joined the EAA because they needed someone who could translate English. Six years later he had become Kenya's clearest and most eloquent voice for cultural nationalism. The KCA saw what they had in Kenyatta even before he started *Muigwithania.* In 1927 they asked him to become their general secretary.

It meant giving up his government job and the good life that went with it. It meant giving up the safety of a part-time club-member for the dangers of a full-time political agitator. Kenyatta knew the government was already keeping its keen eye on him, and he remembered what had happened to Harry Thuku. But here was a chance to do something substantial, and he was still more Kikuyu than European, more Kenyatta than Johnstone. He took the job in 1928.

The decision was to cost him more than he could possibly have guessed. But it was to cost England far more.

> *There was a curious tension everywhere: the very air seemed electric with evil, and it was as if we were encompassed about and beset by unseen forces of darkness on this their own ancient vantage ground. It was a strange occult experience.*
>
> —MRS. HENRY E. SCOTT
> British missionary in colonial Kenya, describing her perception of the native culture she hoped to convert

During the early 20th century the nomadic, cattle-
herding Masai were forced by the British to leave
their traditional holdings. When driven from these
new territories a few years later they applied for help
to the courts, only to be refused a regular hearing on
the grounds that they were not British subjects.

6

Witness

While Kenyatta was cautiously hinting at nationalism in his journal, the Indians in Kenya were openly protesting their treatment by the settlers. They wanted a new constitution and some representation on the legislative council, and they kept up a steady stream of demands to London. Finally, the protest reached such a point that the British government felt it had to appoint a commission to investigate and report on the situation.

The Hilton Young Royal Commission began holding hearings in Nairobi the year Kenyatta accepted the job as general secretary of the KCA. The president of the KCA, Joseph Kangethe, had been imprisoned for two years, so Kenyatta was the acting leader of the association, and when the commission began he determined that the KCA would get a hearing too. Although the commission had come to consider the case of the Indians, Kenyatta was so persuasive that they agreed to hear the complaints of the Kikuyu as well.

As Kenyatta wrote later, he was the natural choice to present the Kikuyu case. "The rules governing land tenure," he wrote in 1938, "were taught to me by my father, who is a landowner. As I was his first son, he was careful to give me all the necessary information. . . . In this way I acquired the knowledge which is a normal part of every Kikuyu education." One of the few Kikuyu fluent in English, he was selected without challenge.

Kenya would be a paradise if the Europeans went back where they came from. Don't think I don't like the English. I do like them—in England. Where they will all soon be.
—JOMO KENYATTA

Kenyatta left Kenya for London from East Africa's principal port, Mombasa, the main street of which still shows the architectural influence of its former Portuguese overlords. Mombasa, originally settled by Arabs in the 11th century, was later a center of the slave trade.

In 1929, just before leaving for London to represent the Kikuyu Central Association, Kenyatta posed for this portrait with his son, Peter Muigai. By this time Peter had a one-year-old sister named Margaret.

Of course the first issue was the land—the central concern of the KCA—but Kenyatta organized a much more complex and comprehensive presentation. He knew that this was a rare opportunity to be heard, and he took advantage of it to present all the complaints of his people.

Along with protection from, or at least fair compensation for, the appropriation of Kikuyu land, Kenyatta made other demands. Among the most important were:

—that the cultural identity of the Kikuyu be recognized and acknowledged by publishing all laws that governed them in the Kikuyu language;

—that the unity of the tribe be maintained by the election of a single "paramount chief," with the authority to try legal cases among the Kikuyu;

—that the Kikuyu be given a chance to make themselves economically independent, and therefore safe from forced labor, by being permitted to grow cash crops like coffee;

—that the I.D. cards be abolished;

—that schools be opened for the natives; and

—that natives have representation on the legislative council.

Farmers carry to market their crops of gourds, fruits whose dried shells are used as bottles or dippers. During the 1920s and 1930s the right of Kenya's natives to decide for themselves which crops to raise became a most important issue for the fast-emerging native political movement.

Kenyatta's presentation hit just the right note, and the time was evidently right for such demands. The results were a triumph for the KCA, and marked the beginning of the end of European domination of East Africa.

The Hilton Young Royal Commission had no authority to grant demands or change laws. It had been appointed only to examine the problems of East Africa and make a report. But the report, issued in January 1930, influenced British government thought profoundly.

The commission report was cautious in its recommendations and took into account the demands or suggestions of all the many groups that appealed to it. It was a balanced, reasonable statement of what seemed fair and possible for the colony in East Africa. Of all the groups that appeared before it—the settlers, the Indians, the Kikuyu, the other tribes—it was the Kikuyu that came out best. And it was the settlers that came out worst.

First of all, the commission stressed the need for cooperation and urged "an equal franchise with

Masai shepherds guard their flocks in a lush mountain valley in Kenya during the 1930s. The Masai, who never settled in villages or towns, roved constantly for centuries, herding their cattle, sheep, and goats over thousands of acres of open grazing country.

Resting Masai warriors remain ready for action, never relaxing their grip on their formidable spears. Skilled at raising livestock, the Masai were also very gifted fighters, much feared throughout southeastern Africa by whites and other blacks alike.

no discrimination between the races." The franchise—the right to vote—belonged at that time to less than 1% of the population of Kenya.

The native races, the report continued, must be "adequately represented" in the government until they are able to take a share in the legislature "equivalent to that of the immigrant communities." The settlers' demand for an independent government—a white nation in black Africa—was effectively denied. At best the Europeans and Indians might stay as equals, not as masters. It was a blow to their status from which the European settlers were never to recover.

In the next year, the British government made several decisions in favor of the natives. Churchill, the colonial secretary, ordered that a parcel of land equal in value to the appropriated territories be added to the Kikuyu reserve. Harry Thuku was released, although on closely supervised parole and with a promise not to engage in any unlawful agitation. The spirit of reform was in the air, and it appeared that England was beginning to move at last toward granting its colony independence.

The Indian merchants had not profited much from the investigations of the Hilton Young Royal Commission, and they recognized that their goal of a constitution had not been argued as well as it might have been. Kenyatta's presentation had met with such good response that the idea occurred to a group of Indians that they might call on Kenyatta for his support. Anything he achieved to liberalize the government of the colony would help them just as it would help the native population.

So a group of Indians approached the KCA with the idea of sending Kenyatta to England to continue arguing for a more liberal policy in Kenya, one that respected the rights of all different groups.

The Indian group was a communist organization, and the KCA was reluctant to accept anything from them. But they had long had the idea of having a spokesman in London, and they had to accept help from wherever they could find it. They agreed and proposed the idea to Kenyatta.

Kenyatta knew it meant leaving all he knew—his

home, his wife, his friends—for a new, strange life in a place he had heard of only from teachers. He also knew he did not have much chance of success. When he discussed it with the acting governor of the colony, he was told it would be "wasting money on an expedition that seemed likely to be fruitless." He had no formal credentials. He could not even speak for his tribe, since officially he represented only the 3,800 members of the KCA. But Kenyatta had always found a way, and he was sure of himself. He accepted without hesitation. In December 1928 the KCA had a farewell ceremony for him at which he swore a solemn oath to keep faith with his people and his land.

In February 1929, accompanied by an Indian with the same mission, Mr. Johnstone Kenyatta set out for England to take his people's grievances to the top. The Kikuyu shepherd had come a long way from the village of Ichaweri—and he still had a long way to go.

Tribal leaders in Nairobi wear ceremonial headdress in honor of visiting British dignitaries during the 1920s. On several occasions during this period prominent British visitors declined to meet the natives, preferring to see only the white community.

7

Scholar

The acting governor was right. Kenyatta did not get in to see the colonial secretary in London because he did not have the proper credentials. The under-secretary received him politely and accepted the petition he carried, but nothing came of it.

Kenyatta was able, however, to testify before parliament. The missionaries in Kenya had brought their complaints against the "pagan" Kikuyu coming-of-age ceremonies to the government, and Kenyatta was able to explain the importance of these rituals among his people to the government. Parliament was impressed by this articulate African and decided against the proposed decree outlawing the ceremonies in Kenya.

It was a success to be proud of, but it had not been his primary goal, and it did nothing for the Indians who had paid his way over. He approached other groups for help and support, and found everyone sympathetic and interested but no one helpful. The colonial office continued to refuse to speak with him.

The only group that seemed really concerned was the communist League Against Imperialism, with which his Indian companion from Kenya had connections. This London-based group accepted him eagerly as a responsible voice against imperialist

W. E. B. DuBois (1868-1963), the black American scholar regarded as the father of Pan-Africanism. A main participant in the 1945 Pan-African Congress (which Kenyatta also attended), DuBois believed that, in a world dominated by European culture and tradition, an "African personality" had to be established before any truly effective political action could occur inside Africa.

Kenyatta was initially dismayed by the huge contrast between England and his homeland: London alone contained more people than all of Kenya, and the weather was cold. "Here," he wrote to his wife in 1929, "the sun is not often seen." He was, however, soon at ease, even adopting a British style of dress.

Huddled beneath a canopy, British noblewomen wait for their chauffeurs following the State Opening of Parliament in London in 1929. Soon after arriving in the British capital, Kenyatta talked to Kenya's governor, Sir Edward Grigg, about Kikuyu land rights. Grigg merely replied that the natives should learn to be patient.

oppression in Africa. They sent him on a visit to Moscow with letters of introduction to leading communists there.

In Russia he was enthusiastically welcomed. Although he did not speak the language and found it difficult to communicate through interpreters, he enjoyed the attention he received. Stalin's Russia in the late 1920s was in a ferment of enthusiasm, and one of the greatest concerns of communism was racial equality. An African who spoke against the injustice of the colonial system was a great favorite with the Russians, and he was well received everywhere. He stayed in Moscow from August to October, but by then the weather was becoming intolerable for an African.

The Russians gave him more introductions to communists in Germany. Kenyatta found the German Communist party fighting for survival against the Nazi party just emerging under Hitler. Again Kenyatta was well received, not as a representative of the Kikuyu tribe, or even of Africa, but as a spokesman for the black race.

He spoke with leading communists in Berlin and went to Hamburg, where he participated in the communist-sponsored International Negro Workers Congress. His magnetic personality and dramatic

Kenyatta met with British colonial undersecretary Drummond Shiels at the Houses of Parliament (on riverbank, at center) in 1930. Although most Colonial Office officials dismissed Kenyatta, Shiels was sympathetic, arguing most prophetically that to "refuse to see or hear emissaries of the discontented" would only drive them toward "violent methods."

Visiting Moscow in 1929, Kenyatta received a warm welcome from communists eager to win over African nationalist leaders. Although impressed by the Soviet Union, whose leaders had proclaimed the dignity and rights of blacks, Kenyatta later recognized much of the Soviets' message as mere propaganda.

Soviet leader Joseph Stalin (1879-1953) addresses workers in 1926. Kenyatta's early admiration for the Soviet system decreased sharply when he discovered, on his 1932 Moscow visit, that the Soviets had reversed a previous policy and now declared that political movements based on race rather than class were a form of "petit bourgeois nationalism."

speaking style made him a popular figure here too, but the conference was set up to support the idea of an international black working class, and that was not what Kenyatta was after. He had come to help his own people, the Kikuyu, and he found little to interest him in international communism.

The sympathy and respect he received were all very well, but he was aware that all of this travel was doing nothing for the cause of justice in Kenya. Kenyatta himself was learning a lot and enjoying himself, but the Indians who had sponsored his trip were becoming impatient. Finally they stopped sending money. The communists enjoyed his interesting presence, but they were not willing to pay for it. So in October 1930 he went back to Kenya.

But just as he had not been able to stay in Ichaweri after he had seen Nairobi, he could not stay in Kenya after he had spent time in Europe. The humiliations of life for a black in Nairobi were especially galling to him now that he had had a taste of the freedom of life in Europe. Somehow he had to get back.

Although the Indians were no longer interested in supporting him, the KCA considered his trip a success. He had made himself heard and seen and fixed the problems of black East Africa in the minds of people in three countries. He had not gotten into the colonial office, but many sympathetic people in London had listened to him and been impressed. In time the doors would open if he kept hammer-

Many Europeans such as these grim-faced Berliners faced unemployment during the Great Depression of the 1930s. Although Kenyatta traveled widely in the Soviet Union in 1932, his hosts insulated him from the realities of life in a country where poverty and famine had combined to kill millions of peasants.

The Lenin School in Moscow, where Kenyatta is said to have taken classes in 1932. At this institute the Soviets educated potential revolutionary leaders in paramilitary tactics, Marxist literature, and political theory. Although Kenyatta responded to the personal warmth of the Soviet people, he had doubts about their government's chosen brand of socialism.

ing at them. Anyway, it was obvious that he could do more for the cause of Kikuyu justice in England than in Kenya. So in July 1930 the KCA brought out a special issue of *Muigwithania* to raise money to send him back to London. He left late in 1931, and he was not to see Kenya again for 15 years.

Kenyatta had almost no money now, but he managed. He did odd jobs, and he lived as cheaply as he could. For part of his first year, he went to school at a Quaker college outside of London, where he worked on his command of the English language. Always involved in politics, he earned a reputation as a radical even while he was studying.

And he kept writing petitions to the colonial office,

which kept ignoring them. The government did not want to consider these questions if it did not have to, and Kenyatta was not an official whose voice had to be listened to. He was merely a poor African student who happened be a member of an obscure political protest group back home in Kenya. London was full of radicals like Kenyatta in those days, and when he stood on a soapbox in Trafalgar Square or Hyde Park making passionate speeches for justice for the Kikuyu, most people saw him as just another harmless crank looking for an audience.

Kenyatta had always gotten a wider audience than most cranks, though, because he had a real issue and the ability to present it convincingly. Already in 1930, before returning to Kenya, he had written a famous letter to *The Times* of London outlining the major demands of the KCA. The letter ended with a warning—not exactly a threat, but a calm prediction of what might happen between England and Africa if these demands were not met. Many people were impressed by this letter, but unfortunately for both the Africans and the English the right people did not take it seriously enough. The colonial office was to look back on this poor African student's warning with regret—after it was too late.

Kenyatta's efforts in these early years in London met with mixed results. He tried to give testimony in a government hearing about a union of East African colonies, but was refused. He succeeded in speaking on Kikuyu land claims to the Carter Land Commission in 1932, and influenced the commission to offer some compensation for lands the settlers had taken. It was not a complete success, though; the commission voted to maintain the policy of restricting the choice highlands area to white settlers, keeping the Kikuyu on overcrowded reserves.

In 1932 Kenyatta visited Russia again, and took some classes at the University of Moscow. There is also a report that he attended the Lenin School, where Mao Tse-tung and other communist revolutionaries had studied. He never admitted this, but there is no question that he learned what he could from the communists without ever committing him-

British author Elspeth Huxley grew up in Kenya and came to be considered an authority on Africa. An unrepentant apologist for British imperialism, Huxley once called Kenyatta "shrewd, fluent, devious, and subtle." In 1953, when Kenyatta was accused of "managing an unlawful society," Huxley branded him "an African Hitler."

A scene from *Sanders of the River*, the 1935 Alexander Korda movie which starred Paul Robeson and also featured Jomo Kenyatta. Although many critics savaged the movie, calling its black participants "white men's niggers" and the film itself contemptuous of native culture, Kenyatta remained unperturbed by this major controversy.

self to their goals. Like the KCA in Nairobi, he took help where he could find it.

Back in London he continued to promote the cause of the native African wherever he could, and supported himself however he could. The flashy dress style of Nairobi gave way to a taste for elegant English suits, and his smooth personal manner enabled him to live well on credit. He was known to have talked his landladies into being patient about the rent.

At one time he shared an apartment with the black American singer Paul Robeson, later in trouble in the United States for his own communist activities. The great singer had crossed the Atlantic to be in a movie where he could play a black man with some dignity, instead of the usual stereotype. In Alexander Korda's 1935 *Sanders of the River* he played an African chief, and succeeded in getting a walk-on part for Kenyatta, who needed the money. Neither of them knew that the editing of the film would make the blacks appear humble and foolish and that the film would be used as an example of the unreadiness of Africans to govern themselves. When Robeson first saw the completed film, he locked himself in his dressing room and refused to appear on the stage.

But Kenyatta did not care much about such things. He was glad of the money, and hoped to get other movie work of the same sort, knowing that

American singer and actor Paul Robeson (1898-1976) performs the title role in the 1933 film adaptation of Eugene O'Neill's play *The Emperor Jones.* Kenyatta first met Robeson in 1930. Discovering that they shared similar views about the need for worldwide unity among blacks, the two men became friends.

We therefore hope that the British people, especially those who believe in justice and fair play, will raise their voice in protest against the repressive policy which the Imperial Government is applying in dealing with their African wards. Even the most elementary democratic rights are denied to native races.
—JOMO KENYATTA
in a letter published by the British magazine *The New Statesman and Nation* on June 27, 1936

The King's Africa Rifles parade in Nairobi during the 1930s. That Africans were conscripted into the British Empire's armies, but not represented on its councils, greatly disturbed many blacks. "Surely," said Kenyatta on one occasion, "if we are considered fit...to fight side by side with whites, we have a right to a say in the running of our country."

the movie image of Africans, which had always been degrading, was an unimportant matter. He talked the film company into letting him keep the costume he had worn, and wore it unabashedly to social events to help publicize his cause. Elspeth Huxley, a British author who supported the white settlers' position in Kenya, called Kenyatta "a showman to his fingertips."

The next year the "showman" did something very undramatic. He signed up for a course in anthropology at the University of London, under Bronislaw Malinowski, probably the leading cultural anthropologist in England. Malinowski was so struck with

Kenyatta's intelligence and insight into the culture of his own people that he arranged a scholarship for him and helped him get a job in the school's department of African languages as an expert on pronunciation.

Three papers Kenyatta delivered in 1936 to a seminar at the School of Economics and Political Science of the University of London particularly impressed Professor Malinowski, and he organized them into a book, for which he wrote an introduction. Kenyatta's *Facing Mount Kenya* was published in 1938, and became a best-seller at once. Although he had never earned an undergraduate degree, he was granted a diploma in anthropology for this work, a pioneering study of African tribal culture.

Facing Mount Kenya is like no other work in anthropology. It was the first major work to study the customs of a "primitive" tribe by a member of the culture. It was an examination "from the inside" by a man who had wide experience of the world and so could see things from both sides. But more unusual than that, it was written by a man deeply committed to certain political and social principles, and the book was as much a work of revolutionary propaganda as of objective scholarship.

It was the tone, rather than the content, of *Facing Mount Kenya* which caused it to be such a bombshell among whites and blacks alike. Its critics called it romantic, sentimental, mystic, and out of date, nostalgically describing the culture of the Kikuyu before they had begun to adapt to European influence. Some critics charged that the book urged a return to primitivism and applauded the dark ways of the past. One missionary wrote, "The author glories in shame and parades that which is indecent."

The settlers in Kenya were even more horrified, seeing the book as a violent attack on the colonial system, and in fact the language often sounds like a communist tract. "The people were put under the ruthless domination of European imperialism through the insidious trickery of hypocritical treaties," Kenyatta wrote. Clearly he was writing a

Jomo Kenyatta's anthropology teacher, Bronislaw Malinowski (1884-1942), considered him an important spokesman for the "educated, intellectual minority of Africans," and helped prepare his book *Facing Mount Kenya*, which asserted that Africans were not savages in need of "Europeanization," but a people whose native culture was as valuable as any in the world.

political testament rather than a scholarly text, but in fact the book has been accepted as both.

In order to give the book an authentic look, Kenyatta had his picture taken for the cover in a borrowed monkey-skin robe, holding a fake spear. To show the people back home that he was still a Kikuyu after all these years in England, and to add to the romantic appearance of being a native, he dropped his missionary name Johnstone for all time and coined the name "Jomo." It had no meaning, but newspapers fixed on the idea that it meant "flaming spear" in Kikuyu, and the idea stuck. "Flaming-Spear" Kenyatta in his robe of a tribal elder, with spear made out of a fence railing, was about as authentic as the "African chief" Robeson had played in *Sanders of the River,* but the public ate it up, and the newly-named Jomo Kenyatta was invited out more than ever. Always the showman, he took advantage of whatever came his way to get his point across.

Ready to return to Kenya now, an international authority on anthropology and a literary celebrity, Kenyatta was stopped by the European outbreak of World War II. The KCA was banned in Kenya by a government that had all it could do to keep the country out of German hands and had no time or patience for potentially subversive organizations inside the country. Kenyatta was cut loose from his African moorings, and the world suddenly lost interest in Kikuyu problems.

He supported himself by lecturing for the Workers Educational Association and working on a farm in Sussex. Popular among the villagers, he got the nickname Jumbo—a play on his new name Jomo and a reference to his size and African origins. He never liked that name, but he got on well with everyone.

In fact, he got on so well with one 32-year-old white woman, a schoolteacher and fellow lecturer, that he married for a third time and fathered another son.

But even during this time of isolation from Africa, Kenyatta kept working for his people. He wrote letters to newspapers and articles for magazines.

Africans who want self-government are always put off with: 'Not yet. Not till you are fit for it.' Certainly we aspire to be fit for self-government. But we should like to know who is to be the judge of our fitness, and by what standards will his verdict be pronounced?
—JOMO KENYATTA
in a letter to the British magazine *The Listener,* August 1943

70

Kwame Nkrumah (1901-1972), later president of Ghana, met Kenyatta at the 1945 Pan-African Congress. Nkrumah, born in Africa's Gold Coast, had studied in the United States, where he joined a black rights movement. Like Kenyatta, he believed in the concept of "Africa for the Africans."

In 1942 he wrote a second book, *My People of Kenya,* and in 1945 a pamphlet, *"Kenya: Land of Conflict,"* repeating and enlarging his 1930 warning in *The Times.*

More important for his image, however, was his work in 1945 just after the war. With American educator W. E. B. Du Bois and future Ghanian president Kwame Nkrumah, he helped form the Fifth Pan-African Congress, in Manchester. It was not a revolutionary movement, and it did not accomplish much of anything, but it was the first effort to unite the leaders of different British African colonies. It gave Kenyatta a reputation at home as something more than a leader of the Kikuyu. When he went back to Kenya in September of the next year, he was ready to lead a truly national party—no longer the Kikuyu Central Association but a new group with wider aims: the Kenya African Union.

He had finished his work in England. A new, unified, postwar Kenya needed him back home. In 1946, leaving his wife and infant son behind in England, "Flaming Spear" set sail for the country he had not seen for 15 years. The native son was going home.

8

Nationalist

Kenyatta returned to a welcome he had never expected. His years away from Kenya had made him feel like a stranger, but the people knew him. He was a legend in Kenya—one of their own who had won the world's respect. No other black African had ever become such a celebrity, and now that he was back none was listened to with more reverence.

He returned as the leader of the Kenya African Union, a group started by Harry Thuku when the KCA was banned in 1940. Like its forerunner, the KAU (which everyone pronounced "cow") was made up mainly of Kikuyu, the largest tribe in Kenya, but an increasing number of members of other tribes were joining every day. Its membership when Kenyatta returned was around 100,000—compared to less than 4,000 members of the KCA when he had left. Each member paid five shillings, about $1.25, a year dues. This was no small amount in a country with an average yearly income below $100.

James Gichuru, the president of the KAU, stepped down for the returning hero, who took office in 1947. Kenyatta was now in effect the leading voice of native Kenya.

When Kenyatta arrived by ship in Mombasa on September 24, 1946, he told the cheering crowd that he had risen at dawn to catch the first sight of Kenya on the horizon. "As soon as I set my eyes on it," he said, with passion, "I felt tears streaming out of my eyes."

Masai warriors, traditionally enemies of the Kikuyu, were at first hesitant about cooperating with other tribes in the Kenya African Union, but Kenyatta worked hard to overcome their resistance. He often began his campaign speeches by saying, "We cannot achieve freedom if it is demanded by one tribe only."

This home of a Nairobi woman and her children reflects a lifestyle common in postwar Kenya. World War II brought prosperity to Kenya's white farmers, but millions of the nation's black residents continued to live in squalor and despair—fertile ground for the seeds of nationalism.

And an eloquent voice it was. Never more a showman than now, his intensely theatrical delivery ignited a fire of enthusiasm in his audiences. Beginning each speech with a long-drawn-out cry of "Eeeeeeh!" which brought a wild burst of applause from his audience, he would launch into a passionate demand for freedom for his people in terms all could understand. The crowds at these rallies were enormous, reaching as many as 50,000 people at one gathering.

He usually spoke in Swahili, the language used

between members of different tribes, but he also spoke some Kikuyu to remind his own people that he had remained one of them. His speeches were at once emotional, angry, and humorous—no one could hear them and remain unaffected. Calling on his listeners to rise above tribal loyalties, he urged unity in their common struggle. For the first time in African history rival tribes like the Masai, the Luo, and the Kikuyu were welded together in a

During the late 1940s many British officials viewed Kikuyu villages like this as possible refuges for secret societies dedicated to the murder of whites. As Kenya's settlers grew increasingly fearful of native hostility, they attributed every crime to such societies, which, by 1948, came to be known as the notorious Mau Mau.

single cause. Jomo Kenyatta was truly a voice for all black Africa.

He had left Kenya a political activist known to the educated few in Nairobi. Now he found himself a new Moses expected to lead his people out of the desert of poverty and oppression to the promised land of freedom.

The natives he saw in Kenya now were different in many ways from those he had left in 1931. From conservative, traditional tribalists, they had become intensely dedicated to the future. Uncertain about where they belonged in the new age, desperate for education, they had a new vision of themselves and their world. During the war, many young men had been drafted into the King's Africa Rifles, an army regiment which had fought outside of Africa. These young men, like Kenyatta, had seen something of the world and had come to realize how oppressed they were in their own country. Returning home to their overcrowded reserves or city ghettos, forced into the most menial jobs when they could get work at all, they felt helpless and frustrated, and turned eagerly to Kenyatta as their savior.

As always, he exerted a special fascination on women. In his middle 50s, he radiated a power and electricity greater than that of many younger men, and his appeal was as great as it had ever been. It was not long before he took his fourth wife, the quiet, sensitive Ngina, with whom he was to have four more children.

With his old friend Mbui Koinange, son of the senior Kikuyu chief and the first African native to earn a college degree in the United States, Kenyatta helped organize and direct the Kenya African Teachers College as an alternative to government schooling, and as a center from which a true nationalist party could grow.

As the principal of the teacher-training college he had organized with Koinange, Kenyatta was in a position to exert an influence on the future of his people. In a short time there were 300 schools in Kenya operating independently of either the colonial government or the missions. They were badly

The purpose of the KAU is the biggest purpose the African in Kenya has, and it is their mouthpiece which asks for freedom.

—JOMO KENYATTA
speaking at a rally in Nairobi in 1947

underfinanced, they did not have enough teachers or money or supplies, but they held 60,000 students eager for education. Kenyatta's school, the Kenya Teachers Training College, was turning out teachers for them as fast as it could, teachers steeped in the native traditions of the Kikuyu. With the support of the KAU and the people, they worked hard to undo what the missionaries had been doing for almost half a century—making the African ashamed and contemptuous of his own culture.

Leading British settler Lord Waterpark surveys a portion of his 750,000-acre ranch in 1961. Kenya's white farmers resisted all efforts of the native population to gain independence. In 1950, a spokesman for the European settlers said, "We are here to stay and the other races must accept that premise with all it implies."

British settlers in Kenya often brought English tradition with them, as evidenced by this 1953 photograph of Lord and Lady Waterpark dressed for dinner. Both whites and blacks considered Kenya a "paradise," but similarities ended there. Kenya *would* be a paradise, Kenyatta said in 1948, "if the Europeans went back where they came from."

Kenyatta traveled extensively during this period, but his home was back in his old village of Ichaweri, where he had a new house built facing Mount Kenya. Here he once again hoed a little garden and lived as peaceful a domestic life as his important duties permitted him.

But he knew that his days of peace and the days of peace for his country were numbered. He tried to steer a moderate path toward independence, but he could feel the pressure of his people for faster progress, and he could hear the drums in the forest.

The colonial government never gave in on anything unless impelled to do so. The settlers' organization was fighting every concession, and generally winning. The KAU continued trying to chip away at the color barrier and to wheedle government support for native education, but it seemed every small success was balanced by an equal failure. The government never really tried to understand the minds of people it considered "only 50 years out of the trees," so it was no wonder that secret societies, always a great tradition among the Kikuyu, began to spring up here and there.

The outlawed KCA had not completely disappeared, and as its imprisoned members were released they set up new branches, working secretly within the KAU and the labor unions. Other secret societies, impatient with the lack of reform and frustrated by their position in a white society, formed spontaneously. Soon it was clear to everyone but the government that trouble was brewing. The fuse seemed to be growing shorter. Even Europeans could feel the tension in the air and knew that it would not be long before the explosion Kenyatta had threatened in 1930 came about.

Europeans relax in a Nairobi cafe in 1962. The white settlers, many of whom were aristocrats, considered Kenya the most fashionable of the British colonies, believing it a land that was meant for perpetual rule by white men.

9

Terrorist

Reform was slow, and the old problems persisted. The government finally relented and allowed natives to grow cash crops, but the Kikuyu were slow to take advantage of the privilege. Changes in work and living habits were not easy to make, and natives disagreed on what to accept and what to reject of modern customs. Some wanted all the advantages of the 20th century at once and resented the delays. Others wanted a return to the simple pastoral life of the past. Postwar unemployment reached 20%, and 22,000 homeless blacks roamed the streets of Nairobi.

The government set up projects to provide work, but the jobs often paid so little or were so objectionable to the culture of the natives that people refused them. In 1947 women walked off a government farming project after a KAU meeting, and other strikes followed. At one strike, police intervened and nine workers were gunned down.

Kenyatta worked openly. He promoted self-improvement and gradual peaceful reform. He was a mature, moderate force, patiently negotiating with administrators and playing a fatherly role with his people. He urged them to pull themselves up by work and education, and scolded them for not growing coffee now that they had finally won the right.

But like his friend Kwame Nkrumah, who went back to the Gold Coast (later Ghana) in 1947, he

Mau Mau? What is that? I have no idea what Mau Mau is. I don't even know what language it is, and I know quite a few African languages.
—JOMO KENYATTA
responding to hecklers while addressing a KAU meeting in Nairobi in February 1951

Jomo Kenyatta attends the Pan-African Congress in Manchester, England, in 1945. He carried many of the Congress's ideas back to Kenya, where he lectured widely on the critical importance of education and hard work. "If we use our hands," he said in 1948, "we shall be men."

British troops check an African's identification papers in Nairobi in 1963. While outside of Nairobi and Kikuyuland the Mau Mau emergency had little effect on everyday life in Kenya, hair-trigger tension prevailed in the city. Assassination of Africans was common, and Europeans carried loaded guns everywhere.

found so much discontent among the people that no one had the patience for his ideas of gradual self-improvement. Rebellion was in the air, especially among the World War II veterans, who had learned skills they could not now employ and had enjoyed a higher standard of living than they could now achieve.

One group of young men, the Kikuyu age-set who had come of age in 1940, became a sort of gang. The "40 Group," as they were called, was composed mainly of ex-servicemen who had fought in Ethiopia, India, and Burma, and were a particularly aggressive crowd.

The colonial government never adapted to new conditions. They continued to believe that the answer to all problems was economic growth under European leadership and tighter police action. But the more the English tried to clear the city of the homeless and unemployed, driving them back to their overcrowded reserves, the more the city's underprivileged wanted to clear the country of the English. Kenyatta could not ignore this group, and increasingly his public addresses began to center around the idea of "Africa for the Africans."

The angry native populace of Kenya and the greedy, insensitive government were on a collision course. Kenyatta tried to avert the tragedy, but it was just a matter of time before the clash. And inevitably he was caught between the two forces.

The 40 Group, engaged in violent political extremism under the name of the Gikuyu Maranga African Union, was joined by a new religious sect called *Dini ya Jesu Kristo.* Members reverted to wearing skins and carrying bows and arrows. Soon these groups generated others like them—fanatics and thugs, criminals and vagrants, sincere political dreamers and desperate people without work or hope. By the late 1940s they were beginning to fuse into a more-or-less unified movement, and Kenya and the world became aware of a terrible new force—the mysterious secret society known as Mau Mau.

No one knows the origin of Mau Mau, or even what the name means. There are many theories.

A Kenyan policeman investigates a chilling sight in 1952: a strangled cat hanging in an arch carrying a Mau Mau message threatening death to any native "who continues to work for the Whites." Although he never publicly endorsed Mau Mau, Kenyatta was jailed for nine years on suspicion of involvement.

British prime minister Winston Churchill, a conservative and dedicated imperialist, fell from power in 1945, to the delight of the Pan-Africanists and the dismay of Kenya's white settlers. His successor, Clement Attlee (1883-1967), favored gradual independence for Britain's colonies, a view which the reactionary settlers considered communistic.

> Our objective here in Africa is justice, after long years of desolation, exploitation and neglect. Africa is fast awakening, not for conquest or disruption or revenge, but to contribute to the world a new philosophy. All men are equal. All men are equally entitled to respect. The talents and resources of the world are enough to banish squalor, and to bridge the gap between the richer nations and those where poverty has stifled man's creativeness.
> —JOMO KENYATTA

Some say the terrorist group began on the Mau Summit. Others think the name was an imitation of a lion's roar with which the *Dini* began its ceremonies. The Gikuyu Maranga African Union dropped the first word of its name, and the initials of the remainder were the MAU. The Kikuyu word for "oath" is "muma," which may have been misunderstood as "Mau Mau." Other explanations are that "Mau Mau" is a form of a Kikuyu slang word meaning "greedy eating," or that the words come from the initial letters of the words of a Kikuyu motto meaning "Let the Europeans return to En-

Suspected Mau Mau terrorists are taken away for police questioning in Nairobi. In 1952, after months of murder and other violence, the government signed an emergency proclamation authorizing widespread arrests of suspected Mau Mau activists. One of them was Kenyatta, whom the authorities apprehended on October 21, 1952.

gland so the Africans may get freedom." Still another explanation is that "Mau Mau" was a rearrangement of the letters of "uma uma"—Kikuyu for "get out."

Whatever the name's origin, it was first heard by police in 1948 and first mentioned in a newspaper in 1950. No one was sure just what Mau Mau was at first—a new religious cult, an underground political party, or a criminal gang. But there was no question about its objectives—to drive the Europeans out of Kenya and to give the Kikuyu control of the country.

The name became an umbrella which covered every anti-government act. Every act of violence was credited to Mau Mau, and every criminal who got caught claimed he was acting on its behalf. The government became alarmed. It could not pin anything down, but it could see that public opposition had found a focus.

Kenyatta's actions were watched carefully, and

he was urged to throw his influence against the movement. He responded with characteristic caution, even after Mau Mau was officially outlawed in 1950. He never even admitted to being aware of the movement, slyly making fun of the question when asked about it.

But he could not laugh off either the atrocities committed by Mau Mau or the government's harsh reprisals. In the first months after banning Mau Mau in August 1950, the police closed down the Kikuyu Independent Schools Association for its supposed "connection with Mau Mau" and arrested 150 natives. But this was like putting up a roadblock against an invading army. By 1951 the estimated membership of Mau Mau was nearly a quarter of a million.

Kenyatta was little help to the government. When ordered to speak against Mau Mau, he continued making veiled, ambiguous statements which could

Edna Kenyatta, who married Jomo in 1942, smiles up at their nine-year-old son, Peter, in England in 1952. Although Kenyatta had not seen his English family for 10 years when he wrote to Edna from prison in 1956, he and Edna had continued to exchange correspondence after his departure. Edna and Peter were honored guests at Kenya's independence celebration in 1963.

A Mau Mau terrorist is captured by soldiers, as another lies dead at right. To overwhelm the estimated 15,000 terrorists who had dispersed into the mountains, the government deployed 11 infantry battalions, 21,000 policemen, and 25,000 members of the Kikuyu Home Guard, who were recruited from villages of "loyal," or anti-Mau Mau, Africans.

not be interpreted as either support or condemnation. And he never stopped insisting that Africa really belonged to the Africans.

The government could do nothing either to make him speak out clearly against Mau Mau or to shut him up altogether. It was afraid to arrest so popular a figure, remembering what happened when Harry Thuku was arrested.

But the pressure was becoming too great to ignore. It was suggested that the communists were supporting the terrorist movement—indeed some

thought that it was "an African communist unit" in the international revolution. Mau Mau was growing larger and bolder, stealing arms and committing acts of sabotage against white settlers' farms. Houses and crops were burned and livestock maimed. Natives loyal to the settlers were killed and often horribly mutilated as a threat to others.

In 1952 Kenya received a new governor from England. Sir Evelyn Baring was a tough, no-nonsense type who did not believe in the gentle approach. He felt that the problem with Kenya had been that the government had not taken a firm enough stand. He was determined to establish his complete authority at once. Within two weeks of his arrival, he sent back to England for military reinforcements and declared a state of emergency. Before it was announced, to be on the safe side, he issued warrants for the arrest of the six leaders of the KAU.

The police thought to take Kenyatta by surprise, but he was waiting for them. When they kicked in the door of his Ichaweri house before dawn on October 21, they found him dressed in the lumber jacket he wore when he spoke in public, holding his hands out for the handcuffs. "What kept you?" he asked with a smile.

Kenyatta had seen this coming and had chosen not to run. He hoped for justice in the courts and had faith in his record for moderation and his own eloquence to save him. It was a costly error in judgment, but not so costly as the government's error in arresting him was finally to prove.

The KAU leaders were only the first to be arrested. Next came the arrests of the heads of the African religious bodies and trade unions. Then the mass arrests began. It was like Nazi Germany. In a few months, concentration camps held more than 50,000 Kikuyu, their land and livestock and cash savings confiscated. All independent schools were closed.

Baring showed who was in charge, but the response was catastrophic. If the Mau Mau had been a formless body, more an angry mob than an organization, as some said, these measures welded it

British administrator Sir Evelyn Baring. As governor of Kenya in 1952, Baring was responsible for proclaiming the state of emergency under which Kenyatta was arrested and jailed. Years later, when Kenyatta was Kenya's president and Baring head of the Commonwealth Development Corporation, Kenyatta maintained cordial relations with his former opponent and persecutor.

Royal Air Force ground staff load a 1,000-pound bomb onto a plane in Nairobi in 1953. Although the British deployed several squadrons of bombers against Mau Mau guerrilla strongholds, the raids had little effect because the heavily forested mountains provided excellent cover for the fugitive terrorists.

into a furious army of rebellion. Baring had declared a state of emergency, but the people of Kenya saw it as a declaration of war. And half a century of oppression had made them ready for it.

The trial of Kenyatta took five months, from December 1952 to April 1953. It attracted international attention, and was generally regarded as a mockery of justice, using the forms of law to get rid of a threat to the government. Kenyatta argued eloquently that the KAU, "which worked in daylight," had nothing to do with Mau Mau, "which struck by night," but the judge did not even listen. Someone was needed to satisfy the settlers that the government was taking care of them, and Kenyatta was the obvious man. On the testimony of paid informants, some later proved to have committed perjury for money, Kenyatta was convicted of "managing Mau Mau," and given the maximum legal sentence of seven years in prison.

The prosecution insisted that this had been a simple criminal case, "the same as if (it) were for picking a pocket," the Crown Counsel claimed. "To describe it as a state trial would invest it with a halo it does not really possess."

But Kenya saw it otherwise, and its immediate result was to unleash a savage reaction from Mau Mau. At the time Kenyatta was sentenced, torture, death, and mutilation were common. Novelist Graham Greene, writing in the *Sunday Times* of London, described "the burnt huts, the charred corpse of a woman, the body robbed of its entrails, the child cut in two halves across its waist, an officer found still living by the roadside with his lower jaw sliced off, a hand and a foot severed."

The government could do nothing but come down ever harder on the natives. And the harsher the punishment, the more bloodthirsty the reaction. A police state developed that undid all the progress toward cooperation between the races. It was estimated that over 90% of the Kikuyu, and a large number from other tribes, belonged to Mau Mau.

Governor Baring and the court had done what even Jomo Kenyatta had been unable to do. They had unified the quarrelsome tribes of East Africa into a common cause.

> *One of the great affronts to human dignity, which I have always opposed, is that of racialism. Never a rational attribute of mankind, this has become an engineered burden on the whole cause of humanity, inflicted by the weakness of arrogance, by opportunities for rewarding domination, and by its effectiveness as a tool of political intrigue.*
> —JOMO KENYATTA

British author Graham Greene (b. 1904), who specializes in novels dealing with political terrorism. Also an essayist, journalist, and travel writer, Greene was appalled by the atrocities he observed in Kenya during the Mau Mau emergency in the 1950s.

10

In Absentia

From 1952 to 1959, Kenyatta was silent. The world heard nothing of him and, in his prison camp in the little desert town of Lokitaung, he heard very little of the world. He was, as he recounted later, "a mere convict, known by number, not by name." His 60s passed slowly as he read books about religion, played checkers, and brawled with his fellow prisoners.

These were the worst years of his life, physically and psychologically. Already past the lifespan of the average African of his time, the old man lived in fear of the snakes and scorpions which infested the camp. He also had reason to fear his English jailors, who constantly threatened to kill him. Once he was ordered to dig what he was told was his own grave. It is not surprising that he turned to drink, seeing no hope for survival.

They were not very good years for his country, either. Kenya was deteriorating as fast as Kenyatta. Where he might have been a voice for moderation, Mau Mau became an epidemic. In 1953 the government banned KAU and the next year arrested more than 160,000 Kikuyu "on suspicion." Civil rights disappeared. In 1955–56, nearly one half of Kenya's entire budget was spent on prisons and police. Kenya was threatened with financial, as well as moral, bankruptcy.

Margaret Wambui, one of Jomo Kenyatta's daughters, calls for the release of her father in 1960, when the great nationalist was still in detention. Margaret, born in 1928, saw little of Kenyatta when she was a child, but later became his closest confidante. The two corresponded regularly while he was in prison.

Masai warriors examine a copy of the first newspaper written in their language. Despite the chaos produced by the Mau Mau uprising, Kenya continued to make cultural and economic progress. Between 1952 and 1959, the nation's European population grew 63 percent and the enrollment of African children in schools doubled.

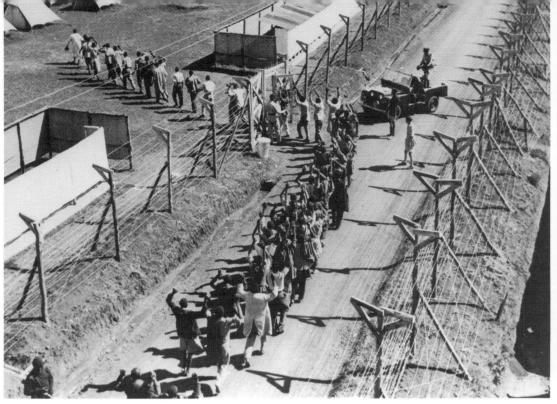

Captured Mau Mau terrorists are marched into the Langata detention center near Nairobi in 1954. Some 80,000 people, most of them Kikuyu, were interned in such camps. It was later revealed that many died in the makeshift prisons, mainly due to the more violent counter-terror measures which were taken by government forces.

For much of the country, Kenyatta remained the leader, even though he was in prison. The government tore down his house in Ichaweri and built an experimental farm there, but the natives continued to treat the place as a shrine. Hope for Kenyatta's release never stopped, despite the growing military power of the government.

By 1956 the government had just about stifled Mau Mau, but at a dreadful cost in both money and world respect. During the seven-year "emergency," Mau Mau had taken the lives of only 32 white civilians and 167 security officers, while 11,503 guerrillas had been killed in battle and over 1,000 hanged by government forces.

The eight armies of Mau Mau had been destroyed, but everyone knew that things could never be the same in Kenya again. Pressures were building up, outside the country as well as inside. Elsewhere in Africa, freedom was in the air. One by one, African countries were gaining independence: Morocco and Tunisia in 1956; Ghana, under Nkrumah, in 1957. And protests from England were adding to the pressure on the colonial government to relax the tight grip in which it held the colony.

Hope began to return to Kenyatta. In 1958, in his middle 60s, he completely gave up not only drinking but even smoking, in preparation for a return to life. The winds of freedom had reached all the way to Lokitaung.

Great changes were taking place in Nairobi, as well. Under liberal pressure, the government opened the legislative council to free elections, and in 1957 black representation equalled white. KAU was legalized again and renamed Kenya African National Union to emphasize its nationalist goals. KANU

In Kenya Colony, the people's leader—Jomo Kenyatta—is jailed. I knew this brave man well in the years I lived in London; like Nehru of India and many others from colonial lands . . . he dreamed of freedom for his people. Well, Nehru was jailed in India . . . but the road to independence and power ran through those prison walls, and Kenyatta too will travel on.
—PAUL ROBESON
in his book *Here I Stand*

Dr. Farnsworth Anderson (at left), director of Kenya's government medical service, accepts a ceremonial doctor's stool from the son of a Luo witch doctor in 1954. Symbolizing the gradual acceptance of European ways by the bulk of the African population, the gift marked the opening of a new health center.

Female members of the Kikuyu Home Guard receive weapons instruction from their village headman in 1955. In their desperation to rid Kenya of terrorism, the British authorities sought to persuade the tribes that Mau Mau could only damage their chances of political advancement.

93

Free at last after nine years in detention, Kenyatta returns to Nairobi in 1961. Greeted by thousands of people, Kenyatta generously showed little bitterness toward his recent captors. He said, "You know the commandment, 'Love thy neighbor,' well, the world is my neighbor."

was a nationalist political party, and its leaders saw Kenyatta as the perfect unifying symbol for it. They declared him the party's president *in absentia* in 1960 and began a campaign for his release.

Although Kenyatta had already been held in detention two years after his sentence had expired, the new governor refused to release the man he called "a leader to darkness and death." But the whole nation took up KANU's cry of *Uhuru na Kenyatta*—Freedom with Kenyatta—and the government could no longer hold back the tide of national sentiment. In August 1961, with bitter forebodings, they opened the gate and let Kenyatta go—to his wife and four children, and to a jubilant rally in Nairobi attended by over 30,000 natives from all tribes. His countrymen were wild with joy and hope. *Mzee*, the Old Man, was back, and *uhuru* was at hand.

Now nearly 70, the old man's powers were undiminished by nine years behind barbed wire in the lifeless northern desert. Despite rumors of his feebleness and uncertainty, he seized the reins of

KANU handed over by fellow Kikuyu James Gichuru and guided it surely toward his goal—*uhuru.*

The path to freedom was still not a smooth one. Naturally the colonial government, hoping to put off the inevitable and still sure that natives were "not yet ready," continued to throw every obstacle in the way. And KANU was divided within itself. Gichuru was a loyal friend, but the other two leaders who had organized the party, Tom Mboya and Oginga Odinga, had other ideas. Both Luo tribesmen, they were ambitious, communist-oriented younger men. Kenyatta knew he could not do without them, but he could see that he would have trouble with both. Perhaps no one but Kenyatta could have kept the party from flying apart.

But the progress toward *uhuru* was irresistible, and differences of opinion within the party seemed unimportant. KANU had no serious white opposition. Its only rival was another black party favored by the colonial government. Freedom was no longer

This is Jomo Kenyatta speaking from Lodwar.... The time has come when Africa must stand with other nations and show that she has something, not only to receive, but also to give to the world. I hope peace and prosperity will come to our people, when all of us can unite and work for the purpose of uplifting our people who have been struggling so hard for centuries.
—JOMO KENYATTA
in a taped address recorded while he was still in detention and played back to delegates to the All Africa People's Conference in Cairo, Egypt

Jomo Kenyatta and his associate, Tom Mboya, attend the Kenya Constitutional Conference in London in 1962. Prior to Kenyan independence, agreements had to be reached on such matters as safeguards for minorities, military bases, security, and the future of Europeans employed in Kenya's civil service.

an issue, so *Uhuru na Kenyatta* no longer served as a motto. The new rallying cry spoke for the goals of the new, free Kenya: *Harambee.* It was an old Swahili loggers' cry, meaning "Lets pull together!"

Unity was the keyword now—unity of tribes within Kenya and unity of the country with other free African nations. In a tribally diverse land, it was not an easy goal.

Harambee was an inspired and inspiring campaign slogan—later, in fact, it was inscribed on the emblem of Kenya as the country's motto—and KANU was swept into power with it. With a thunderous roar of *Harambee,* the native party took over the government of Kenya at last.

On December 21, 1963, Kenyatta had the pleasure of watching the British flag hauled down and the flag of the new republic of Kenya raised in its place. Black for the people of Africa, red for the blood shed for freedom, and green for the lush hills of the country, the new flag waved proudly as Jomo Kenyatta took the oath of office as the nation's first prime minister.

The beautiful equatorial land of Kenya, larger than France and potentially as rich, had never been a country. The English had created it arbitrarily, its boundaries, like those of most of the new Afri-

Kenyatta points to the flag that will fly over independent Kenya. During the ceremony marking the end of colonial rule, on December 12, 1963, the new flag became momentarily tangled and the duke of Edinburgh, who represented the queen of England, whispered to Kenyatta, "Do you want to change your mind?" The prime minister of independent Kenya simply smiled.

can nations, cutting across tribal lines. Ruling Kenya, as the English had found out, would not be easy. *Uhuru* was just the beginning. Now it was necessary to create a nation. The people of Kenya needed, as Kenyatta declared, "a sense of national direction and identity." The new prime minister made a solemn vow as he took office. He would not, he promised, be a prime minister for the Kikuyu alone. "My work," he said, "is for the African people."

Costumed tribesmen dance in celebration of Kenya's independence. Thousands attended the solemn ceremony at which Queen Elizabeth's husband, the duke of Edinburgh, handed over to Kenyatta the formal documents that granted the nation freedom.

97

11
Statesman

Drawing and holding Kenya together was the first and greatest job of the new government. Civil wars—tribal and regional—had rocked most emerging African nations, and Kenyatta was determined that this would not happen to his.

He began by persuading the opposition party to join KANU, and thus making himself the president of a one-party country in 1964. His opponents called it the beginning of a dictatorship, but Kenyatta saw the move as necessary for two reasons. First, it effectively put an end to tribal conflicts at the national level, since separate political parties tended to form along tribal lines. Second, it ended the danger that other countries would try to influence Kenya's politics by playing one party against the other. The magic cry of *Harambee* convinced the nation. Kenyatta had won the respect and support of American presidents Kennedy and Johnson, and he was shrewdly determined to keep the good will of Russia as well.

Kenyatta skillfully kept his country balanced between the East and the West in world politics. With

Freedom came to us through AFRICAN UNITY. It was all of us being united: those in prison camps and detention camps, in the towns and in the country.... All we Africans were in a state of slavery, and all of us together brought our freedom.
—JOMO KENYATTA
speaking in Nairobi on Kenyatta Day,
October 20, 1967

Confronted by enormous challenges, President Kenyatta continued to hold few grudges and made practical use of available resources. Recognizing the importance of law and order, he declined to reorganize the army and police after independence; he also retained many skilled white judicial and civil service officials in the most senior managerial positions.

Jomo Kenyatta whirls a dancing partner during a pre-independence party at his farm in 1963. The Kenyan leader's legendary energy never deserted him.

the dexterity of a juggler, he avoided taking sides with either major power. In time, he was to lead the African countries in forging a solid bloc of nonaligned nations.

The policy of nonalignment had been the official position of his party, a part of the manifesto upon which KANU was elected to power, but once it began to go into operation it was to be the opening wedge that split his government. The vice president, Oginga Odinga—one of the men who had campaigned for Kenyatta's release from detention—wanted closer ties with Russia and finally broke with the government to form his own party. "Workers . . . have been losing hope that this is a government for the working people, and one in touch with their needs," he wrote in 1967. But *Mzee* was too solidly placed in the people's heart to be much affected. "If you play around with me, Odinga," he announced, "you'll be playing around with a lion!"

The spirit of *Harambee* pervaded everything in his government. If it made him a dictator, unwilling to tolerate opposition, it also made him the most democratic president in Africa, determined to end all tribal, class, and racial conflict. "People of different races, colors, and religions can walk together to build a new Kenya, a new nation," he said.

The first and most daring act of the new president was to welcome the frightened whites to stay in the country. It was an amazing act of faith in the future, for a country that had been torn with racial bitterness.

He knew that if the big farms the white settlers had operated so profitably for half a century were snatched by angry natives and broken up into little patches, Kenya would soon revert to a primitive stage of subsistence farming. He also knew that if the hated whites were driven out and the envied Indians made to give up their businesses, no foreign capital would be invested in Kenya, and the country would sink back into the past.

So after 50 years of oppression, after the nightmare of Mau Mau, after nine years of personal suffering in the white man's prisons, Kenyatta held out his hand for reconciliation without rancor. "We must try to trust one another," he said. "Stay and cooperate."

The world watched with wonder as this most violent of countries, born in the flames of terrorism and death, became a model of harmony. Among the dictatorships of Africa, only Kenya was able to support a free press, public health service, and education. Drawn by the high degree of personal freedom and security, foreign investments began to come and the economy flourished.

And where the English had allowed primitive tribes to be visited as "human zoos" for the amusement of European tourists, Kenyatta's government helped to raise all the people of Kenya to an equal level. "The colonialists did not do much to help the Masai," he admitted in 1964. "They just left them like game for people to come and take their pictures." Under Kenyatta, the insulting life of those days was over at last.

It was no easy task to modernize a nation without violating its traditions. Kenyatta had seen and

Arrayed in an opulent leopardskin cloak and carrying his traditional silver fly whisks, Kenyatta presides over ceremonies in Nairobi marking the second anniversary of Kenya's independence. Seated with the president are Oginga Odinga (at left) and Minister of Security and Defense Njoroge Mungai.

Jomo Kenyatta and Israeli Foreign Minister Golda Meir exchange views as ground is broken for a new Israeli embassy in Nairobi in 1963. Although he received many distinguished foreign guests in Kenya, Kenyatta—except for a single trip to an international conference in London—never left Africa after he gained the presidency.

fought bitterly against the mistakes the European missionaries had made, and he was not likely to make the same ones. Yet he was dedicated to eliminating those superstitions that were holding his people back. He never ceased to speak against witch doctors who took advantage of the ignorance of natives. Perhaps no one but the revered *Mzee*, himself the grandson of a Kikuyu magician, could have made fun of witch doctors without angering his listeners in Kenya.

Time magazine told a story, after his death, of how he handled trouble in his government. A minister on his staff was suspected of corruption, and *Mzee* called him into his private office. "Come sit by me, close," he said. "What is your name?"

When the frightened minister answered, Kenyatta struck him sharply across the head with his heavy wooden walking stick. Then he asked again, "What do people call you?" At last the unhappy official admitted that he was called "Mr. Ten Percent" because of the ten-percent kickback he took in giving government contracts. "No more!" cried Kenyatta, and hit him again, twice. That official never strayed again.

With the passing years, Kenyatta's presence became almost legendary. The motorcycle of his early days in Nairobi gave place to a Rolls Royce, and the lumber jacket was replaced by a sharply tailored English suit—blue pinstripe was his favorite—but he still wore the beaded *kenyatta* around his waist, a reminder of his origins. On his head he wore the bright cap of a Luo chief, a gift from that tribe. Wearing emblems of the two principal tribes—long rivals in Kenya—was a public sign that the government, in the person of Jomo Kenyatta, was for all tribes equally.

To the rest of the world, Kenyatta was a symbol of even more. He became the personification not

Visiting Moscow in 1964, Kenyan vice - president Oginga Odinga presents the Soviet premier, Nikita Khrushchev (1894-1971), with a gift from Jomo Kenyatta—a sword and sheath "made by Kenyan patriots." Although Kenyatta eagerly accepted aid from both capitalist and communist countries, he sternly forbade communist activities in Kenya.

A Bible in one hand and a ceremonial whisk in the other, Kenyatta takes office as president of Kenya—now a republic within the British Commonwealth—on the first anniversary of independence. Administering the oath of office, resplendent in full British judicial regalia, is Kenya's chief justice, Sir John Ainley.

only of his own country, but of the new Africa, and of the peaceful transition from colonialism to independence. Under his strong hand, Kenya grew rich. Foreign investors, impressed with the peace of the country and the stability of its government, expanded the agricultural resources and created industry. Exports of coffee, chemicals, and hides have brought in machinery in exchange. And the beautiful climate and scenery and great game preserves of the country have made Kenya one of the world's foremost tourist attractions.

For 14 years, *Mzee* guided his nation as president. There were scandals in his last years—his ambitious rival Tom Mboya was mysteriously killed in 1969, for example, and Kenyatta's large family assumed more and more power in the country—but the beloved Old Man weathered every storm. His personal wealth was said to be enormous. He and his fourth wife controlled the gambling casinos in Nairobi, and had a hand in most industries. They also held huge farming tracts—the dream of all Kikuyu. But the people of Kenya were loyal to him to the end. He began his life as a shepherd, and so he remained, leading his flocks through the perils of the 20th century as surely as he had once led his father's goats in the highlands facing the sacred mountain.

He called himself a lion when he challenged his disloyal vice-president, but in truth Jomo Kenyatta was no lion. He was a fox. Lions are powerful and

Following his 1964 presidential inaugural, Kenyatta reviews his troops. Never hesitant to use British expertise when it suited his purposes, Kenyatta retained many British army officers. Shortly after Kenya had gained independence, he called in British troops to deter a threatened rebellion by one of his own army units.

A policeman wades into a crowd of job-seekers in Nairobi in 1970. Although Kenyatta's skillful handling of the national economy brought considerable prosperity to his underdeveloped nation, unemployment always remained a persistent problem. One relief measure ordered by Kenyatta in 1970 was a significant increase in general recruitment to the Kenyan civil service.

Thousands of grieving Kenyans wait their turns to view the body of their beloved Jomo Kenyatta on August 24, 1978. The deaths of few other African leaders have drawn such a massive outpouring of genuine affection and sorrow as did that of Jomo Kenyatta, who died at age 84 on August 22, 1978.

frightening, but the young Kamau had speared them when they raided his father's herds. Foxes survive, and so did Kenyatta. In his middle 80s, loved and honored throughout the world, the Flaming Spear of Kenya died peacefully in his bed.

He left behind a rich, peaceful nation, probably the most democratic and stable on the continent. His life had spanned the whole period of colonialism in Kenya; he had seen the English in and out. When he died on August 22, 1978, his people mourned him deeply, and the world knew that it had lost a great symbol of freedom. Jomo Kenyatta had done much and suffered much to see his people free, and had lived to lead them into the modern age.

To the sound of muffled drums, Jomo Kenyatta's funeral cortege moves through Nairobi, on August 31, 1978. Perhaps echoing in the minds of the hushed observers were Kenyatta's inspiring words: "I have always stood for the purposes of human dignity in freedom, and for the values of tolerance and peace."

Chronology

1894	Born Kamau wa Ngengi, in Ichaweri, near Nairobi, in East Africa
June 1895	Britain establishes the East African Protectorate
1902	First wave of European settlement in Kenya
1905	Kamau first meets Europeans at Church of Scotland mission hospital
1915	Britain issues Crown Lands Ordinance appropriating native holdings throughout Kenya
1920	Britain declares Kenya a colony Kikuyu Association founded in Nairobi
1921	Kamau moves to Nairobi and takes name Kenyatta Young Kikuyu Association and East African Association founded in Nairobi by Harry Thuku
March 14, 1922	Harry Thuku arrested
March 16, 1922	British police fire on native demonstrators protesting Thuku's arrest, killing 25
1925	East African Association disbands and reorganizes as Kikuyu Central Association
1928	Kenyatta becomes general secretary of the Kikuyu Central Association Launches *Muigwithania* and acts as spokesman before Hilton Young Commission
Feb. 17, 1929	Kenyatta departs for London as official representative of the Kikuyu Central Association
Aug.–Sept. 1929	Kenyatta visits the Soviet Union
1936	Kenyatta studies anthropology in London
1940	Kikuyu Central Association banned
1944	Kenya African Union founded
1945	Kenyatta helps institute Fifth Pan-African Congress
Sept. 24, 1946	Kenyatta returns to Kenya as head of the Kenya African Union
1952	Mau Mau rebellion erupts
April 8, 1953	Kenyatta sentenced to seven years in prison
1960	Kenya African National Union founded
Aug. 22, 1961	Kenyatta released from detention
1962	Kenyatta negotiates terms of a Kenyan constitution in London
June 1, 1963	Kenyatta elected prime minister
Dec. 21, 1963	Kenya gains independence
Dec. 1964	Kenyatta becomes president
Aug. 22, 1978	Kenyatta dies, of natural causes, at age 84

Further Reading

Aaronovich, S. and K. *Crisis in Kenya*. London: Lawrence & Wishart, 1947.

Barnett, Donald L. and Karari Njama. *Mau Mau from Within*. New York: Monthly Review, 1968.

Bennett, George. *Kenya, a Political History: The Colonial Period*. London: Oxford University Press, 1963.

Bennett, George and Carl G. Roseberg. *The Kenyatta Election*. New York: Oxford University Press, 1961.

Cox, Richard. *Kenyatta's Country*. New York: Praeger, 1965.

Delf, George. *Jomo Kenyatta: Towards Truth about "The Light of Kenya."* New York: Greenwood, 1961.

Kenyatta, Jomo. *Facing Mount Kenya*. New York: Random House, 1962.

Kenyatta, Jomo. *Harambee! The Prime Minister of Kenya's Speeches, 1963–1964*. New York: Oxford University Press, 1964.

Murray-Brown, Jeremy. *Kenyatta*. London: Allen & Unwin, 1979.

Odinga, Oginga. *Not Yet Uhuru: An Autobiography*. New York: Hill & Wang, 1967.

Slater, Montagu. *The Trial of Jomo Kenyatta*. London: Secker & Warburg, 1955.

Welbourn, F.B. *East African Rebels*. London: Friendship, 1961.

Worsley, Peter. *The Trumpet Shall Sound*. London: McGibbon & Kee, 1967.

Index

Dennis Wepman has a graduate degree in linguistics from Columbia University and has written widely on sociology, linguistics, popular culture, and American folklore. He now teaches English at Queens College of the City University of New York. He is also the author of *Simón Bolívar* in the Chelsea House series WORLD LEADERS PAST & PRESENT.

Arthur M. Schlesinger, jr., taught history at Harvard for many years and is currently Albert Schweitzer Professor of the Humanities at City University of New York. He is the author of numerous highly praised works in American history and has twice been awarded the Pulitzer Prize. He served in the White House as special assistant to presidents Kennedy and Johnson.